Roaring Lions, Cracking Rocks, and Other Gems from Proverbs

Matt —

Congratulations on your book! Hope this one will be an encouragement to your growth in the spirit of Proverbs 4:7.

Warren B
Dec '09

ROARING LIONS, CRACKING ROCKS, AND OTHER GEMS FROM PROVERBS

WARREN BALDWIN

You can keep up with Warren on his personal blog, Family Fountain, at http://warrenbaldwin.blogspot.com/

To order additional copies of this book, contact:
Xlibris Corporation
1-888-795-4274
www.Xlibris.com
Orders@Xlibris.com
56095

CONTENTS

Thanks to Luke Ellsbury of Cody, Wyoming for the mountain lion and cliff photographs used in the cover design. Thanks to Joyce Brom for editorial work on this manuscript. Thanks to Kristi Kunselman for the photo on the back cover.

Thanks to our parents, Warren & (the late) Elaine Baldwin & Donna Baldwin and Jim & Thelma Swails for being examples of Wisdom.

FOREWORD

Proverbs are short, pithy sayings that arrest our interest and demand our attention. They are catchy and memorable, making them easy to transport to new situations. Proverbs can spark lively conversation or intense debate.

Proverbs are all around us, even in the secular world. "If at first you don't succeed, try, try again." "A dollar saved is a dollar earned." "The early bird gets the worm." Such witticisms take years of accumulated wisdom and experience and condense them into short, catchy sayings. These sayings can be memorized and applied to future settings that reflect similar elements. Such truisms become the truth and guiding lights of our lives. Thomas Long, author of Preaching and the Literary Forms of the Bible writes, "The question is not, will people live by proverbs, but what kind of proverbs will they cherish?" (p.55).

Like the secular sayings, the biblical proverbs reflect wisdom and experience, but they offer the added ingredient of divine influence and personality. One purpose of Proverbs is to promote a relationship with God. "Trust in the Lord with all your heart and lean not on your own understanding." (3:5) The real aim of Proverbs is not to equip us with witty sayings to help us function more professionally in the world; it is to promote godly character so that we can enjoy virtuous relationships with God and people.

Proverbs function by stirring our imagination. "Wounds from a friend can be trusted, but an enemy multiplies kisses." (27:6) Is this saying true? Our minds rush to situations in life where a friend hurt our feelings by telling us an uncomfortable truth about ourselves. After the pain of the unwelcome comments faded, we were able to assess their truthfulness and possibly conclude, "My friend was right. I was out of line. I need to conduct myself with more discipline and dignity in the future." Then, our minds may rush to compliments and flattery an "enemy" showered upon us, only to realize later their emptiness. They were not intended to encourage us but to secure some selfish aim for the one offering the praise.

A proverb stirs our imagination by drawing our minds backwards to situations that reflect the meaning of the saying. Our own experience in life confirms its truthfulness. Secondly, a proverb pushes our thinking forward to future situations, arming us with insight into appropriate thinking and behavior (Long, 57).

Here is an example of what I mean. Proverbs 15:17 says, "Better a meal of vegetables where there is love than a fattened calf with hatred." This proverb pushes my mind back to the Vermont farmhouse where I grew up. Our kitchen was small and square shaped and wouldn't accommodate a typical dining room table. So, we used a square-shaped picnic table complete with wooden benches and the occasional splinter. No one minded, not even company. Our home was the gathering spot for family activities and dinner here was the central event of the day. Around the family picnic table my siblings and I learned about history, our family roots, sex and marriage, philosophy of life, and even how to treat a little sister. "Better a meal of vegetables where there is love . . ."

This proverb also pushes my mind back to my college days. At a Friday night devotional I saw a young lady I had known casually for several years. I asked her if she'd like to grab something to eat. In Henderson, TN, there wasn't much available at 10:30 p.m. except a truck stop. Not only were the dining options limited, but my money was as well. We shared an order of Ore Ida Tater Tots and soft drinks. It was simple, relaxing and fun. The young lady seemed happy and accepted what little I was able to provide. I thought, "She is a gem." We have been eating meals together for twenty-seven years now. "Better a meal of Ore Ida Tator Tots where there is love . . ."

When my family traveled to Cody, WY, to interview with a church, I wanted to eat elk meat. A gentleman and his wife prepared a wonderful meal for us, featuring Wyoming elk. We loved not only the delicious food but also the friendly reception we received and the warm conversation around the table. We moved to Cody and this kind couple prepared many more meals for us. "Better a meal of elk with Marion and Violet where love is . . . ."

Many more special meals from the past flood my mind. Bill and Shirley shared their table with me when I was interviewing in Ulysses, KS. A river bank was transformed into a kitchen when George, Ruby and their clan invited my family to frequent fish fries in Florida. My future in-laws, Jim and Thelma, treated me as an honored guest at their table when I called on their daughter and loaded me up with leftovers for my return to graduate school. My fellow members at the church in Ulysses make our Wednesday meals of pancakes and sausages or ham and beans a feast of friendship and fellowship. "Better a meal of hot dogs where there is love . . ."

Sometimes these meals of the past were sumptuous feasts of fine food. Sometimes they were a simple array of common fare. But always they were celebrations of friendship with conversation that bound our hearts together in love. These meals of the past prepare me for future experiences of sharing the table with treasured family and friends. Proverbs 15:17 is right.

The proverbs stir our imagination. In the following pages I share with you how individual proverbs stirred my thinking, and I hope they do the same for you.

Warren Baldwin

HUSBAND AND WIFE

MARRIAGE AS COVENANT

Wisdom will save you from the adulteress . . . who has left the partner
of her youth and ignored the covenant she made before God.
—Proverbs 2:16–17

I don't know anyone who plans on his or her marriage going bad. They don't
plan on losing interest in each other or developing interest in someone else.
When a man and woman marry, they don't plan on stepping out on their
mate, hurting their kids, losing their standing, and breaking numerous
hearts. But it happens.

It may happen because we don't plan on it not happening. We may
just assume that the physical attraction that drew us together and the love
that led us down the aisle would always be there in mega doses to feed our
romance and sustain our bond. Standing at the altar, could we ever project
ourselves forward to the time when we would look at the other and say,
"I don't find you attractive anymore . . . I'm tired of you . . . I don't love
you . . . I want out"? But it happens. The Sage* doesn't want it to. God
doesn't want it to.

Why do people lose interest or intensity of feeling for their mate? It may
be that we don't schedule our time, energy, and thoughts for our spouses.
Rick Atchley wrote,

> Our mates should not get our time, our energy, or our bodies
> after everyone else. Our marriage covenants are supposed to be

earthly illustrations of God's faithfulness to his people, so we
need to make our marriages a priority. (Sinai Summit: Meeting
God with our Character Crisis [Fort Worth: Sweet Publishing,
1993], p. 141)

Haven't we all been guilty of devoting too much time and energy to
"stuff," then coming home too tired to play with our kids and romance our
spouses? Even playing with our children needs to be balanced with the time
we spend in intimate conversation and recreation with our spouses. Jobs,
kids' sports, and chores are all important; but they can become detrimental
to the covenant we entered with God and our husbands or wives. God gives
us the option of quitting one job and going to another if it doesn't meet our
family needs, but he does not give us the option of quitting our marriage
to find another spouse that we think can better adapt to the rigors of our
career demands.

The upward climb of the corporate world may need to be put on hold.
Some sports activities may need to be curtailed. Some jobs around the house
may have to wait a week in the interest of investing time and devotion with
our spouses today. Our spouses need to know they are our top priority.
Rick continues,

> God . . . is concerned about whether you cherish your mate. God
> never calls us to do the minimum possible to follow his teachings.
> God says in the seventh principle (commandment) that he does
> not want us to commit adultery. But on a deeper level it teaches
> that God does want us to do the kinds of things that enhance
> and celebrate our covenant and that communicate that we hold
> it and our partner precious. (ibid.)

Marriage is a covenant. The devotion, friendship, and sexual union
between the husband and wife is a fountain that can continue to captivate
their attention toward each other, quench and refresh their physical needs,
and bless their relationship all the days of their marriage.

* Note: While we believe Solomon wrote many of the proverbs we
know he didn't write them all. In referring to the author of Proverbs some
contemporary writers prefer to use the designation, "the Sage." In this book
I use both Solomon and the Sage.

MARRIAGE VOWS

May your fountain be blessed, and may you rejoice in the wife
of your youth.

—Proverbs 5:18

"Do you promise to forsake all others and keep yourself faithful to her
(him)?" I ask that question at weddings. I never hear anyone say, "Well,
yeah, I guess, at least until someone better or more attractive comes along.
I'll reassess how I feel then."

When I ask, "Do you promise to forsake all others and keep yourself
faithful to her (or him)?" the answer is always the same: "I do." It is always
said with a smile and sometimes even with a tear. I have no doubt that nearly
everyone who says those words believes them.

But those words don't always stick. Too many times "Jack" meets "Jill,"
and in euphoric ecstasy he forgets all about "Jane," the woman to whom he
made his vow. (This can work both ways.) What happened to that euphoric
feeling at the time of the wedding? What happened to the vow?

I wonder if we understand the nature of the vow we make at our
weddings. To whom or to what do we make that vow of faithfulness and
loyalty? Is it to another person, our husband or wife? Or is that vow a
commitment we make to a love feeling? I wonder if, when we say, "I do,"
we aren't really making a vow to the feeling: "As long as I feel this ecstasy,
I'm here. But once the feeling is gone, I will pursue it somewhere else."

No, no one actually says that, and I don't think most even think it. On
their wedding day a young couple can't imagine the intensity of their love ever
diminishing. But it does; and when it does, people do look elsewhere. That is why
I think many people don't have a clear understanding about marital vows.

What is the purpose of the vow? It is to keep us faithful when the feeling
wanes. The purpose of the vow is to keep us coming home to our spouse
even when the ecstasy of love may be gone. That is why we make vows. If
the love feeling was always there, we wouldn't need the vows, would we?
The love feeling by itself would keep us coming home. But over time, as
life wears on and emotions change, the vow keeps us from looking outside
our marriage to rekindle that flame.

We need to understand that the feeling of love cannot go on forever at
a fever pitch. In the best of marriages, emotions rise and fall. Intensity of

passion ebbs and flows. The love feeling can burn hot and then cool off. That's when the intent of the vows kicks in and protects us.

It is not popular to talk of God, Bible, or duty in relation to marriage today; but these are important concepts. God ordained marriage. He made woman as the helpmeet for man. The Bible explains God's high purpose for marriage: to meet each other's needs, to reflect the unity of God, and to bring new life into the world. Duty or obedience is the orienting of our hearts and minds to do what God wants us to do rather than doing what we want to do. Being faithful to our marriage is obedience. Even if we don't understand God's purpose for marriage, we can still use some common sense to figure out that if we jump this marriage for greener pastures, the grass over there could eventually dry up as well. We are best to stay where we are and work on refreshing the relationship here.

The vow keeps us faithful until the time when we realize that the ecstasy of emotion isn't what marriage is ultimately about anyway. Sadly, those who neglect their vow will never experience marriage at this deeper level. Marriage is more about relationship, companionship, and friendship than it is about feelings. Solomon's prayer for his son, "May your fountain be blessed, and may you rejoice in the wife of your youth," is God's concern for your marriage.

PERMANENT FAITHFULNESS

Should your springs overflow in the streets, your streams of water in the public squares? Let them be yours alone, never to be shared with strangers.

—Proverbs 5:16–17

Water is frequently a metaphor in the Bible for sexual relations enjoyed by a husband and wife. In Song of Solomon, a young husband extols his new bride's beauty, drawing images from nature. He tells her, "Your lips drop sweetness as the honeycomb," and "milk and honey are under your tongue." Finally, he tells her, "You are a garden fountain, a well of flowing water" (Song of Sol. 4:15) This young husband delights in the physical beauty of his bride and anticipates the consummation of their love for each other.

In Proverbs 5:15, Solomon encourages a young husband to "drink water from your own cistern, running water from your own well," meaning, to keep your love at home. Your wife is the fountain and well that will quench your thirst.

There is an exclusiveness to the sexual relationship in marriage. This physical connection is never to be shared with another. A young man is to keep himself pure before marriage and certainly afterward. His love and energy are reserved exclusively for his wife, even before he ever meets her! Think how comforting it is to a young wife to know that her husband waited for years, even before he ever met her. She can rest in the confidence that if her husband was faithful to her before they were even married, his faithfulness to her will continue after the vows.

This principle works both ways. I remember a woman saying, "I hate men." She had good reason. A number of men, both husbands and boyfriends, had loved her for a while, then had moved on to other relationships. When the physical connection between them became routine, the men searched for other cisterns. She was hurt. But she could never see that she caused part of her hurt. She, too, participated in behavior that was not exclusive to one man in one marriage. She didn't keep the cistern, her love, exclusive.

There is also permanence to the sexual relationship in marriage. The "streams of water" that satisfy a husband and wife are "never to be shared with strangers." A stranger is anyone foreign to the marriage covenant. The exclusiveness of the relationship helps to build the permanence: one man, one woman, forever. Never should the love be shared with another. As the husband and wife say no to outside intruders to their love, they continue to say yes to each other.

Permanence is a challenge today. We are a "throwaway" culture. We eat our meals on plates with utensils that are all thrown away. No permanence. I even remember reading about a jewelry store that would rent wedding rings! They thought that would have appeal to a culture that sees so many of its marriages lasting only a few years.

There is nothing disposable about a wedding or the married life that follows it. God built permanence into the "I do," and he wants us to honor it. The sexual component of marriage for pleasure and procreation is God's gift to the union. Sexual union is

> the symbol of God's commitment to us, the sign of our covenant promising to our spouse, the expression of our permanent faithfulness. (Marva Dawn, Sexual Character: Beyond Technique to Intimacy [Grand Rapids: Eerdmans, 1993], p. 56)

There is a physical and emotional joy that can be found only in a sexual relationship that is exclusive and permanent. There is no nagging guilt or shame. The openness, truth, and compatibility of such a relationship feed the exclusive and permanent nature of the union, encouraging both partners to continue to drink from their own fountain.

EVIL DEEDS

The evil deeds of a wicked man ensnare him; the cords of his sin hold him fast.

—Proverbs 5:22

I was riding horses with a friend in Cody, Wyoming. We came to a gate, and my friend got off his horse and opened it. The gate was made of several wire strands attached at either end to wooden posts. He undid one post and pulled it back, allowing the wire strands to coil up and our horses to pass through the opening. Some of the other horses in the pasture decided they wanted to go out, too. One of them stepped onto the coil, and when he tried to step out, the coil tightened around his foot. Feeling the tug, he began pulling harder, and the wire cut into his ankle. My friend rushed to the horse to stop him. Hearing his master's voice and feeling his tight grip on his halter made the horse stop so we could untangle him from the wire cords that had ensnared him. But until the horse relaxed and let the wire relax, he was bound tight.

"The evil deeds of the wicked man ensnare him; the cords of his sin hold him fast." This verse appears in a section discussing the tension between moral sin and moral purity. Solomon warns his son to be careful of sexual indiscretion. He says, "May your fountain be blessed, and may you rejoice in the wife of your youth" (Prov. 5:18) and "Why be captivated, my son, by an adulteress? Why embrace the bosom of another man's wife?" (Prov. 5:20) Solomon is saying, "Be happy with the wife you have at home. Keep your love at home. Don't go looking elsewhere for the attention and affection of another woman." Solomon then gives three reasons for his son to stay pure and to abstain from sexual indiscretions.

One, God is watching. "For a man's ways are in full view of the Lord, and he examines all his paths" (Prov. 5:21). This verse is a stern warning: God is watching.

Two, moral sins ensnare you. "The evil deeds of a wicked man ensnare him; the cords of his sin hold him fast" (Prov. 5:22). The evil Solomon is describing here is the man who leaves his wife at home in order to enjoy the company and sexual pleasures of another woman. He may get stuck in this lifestyle. Solomon says that it will bind him like wire bound that horse's foot.

Three, moral sin will kill you. "He (the adulterer) will die for lack of discipline, led astray by his own great folly" (Prov. 5:23). How will he die? Solomon doesn't say here, but we can use our imaginations. With the STDs circulating, who wants to jeopardize his health over an evil deed? Later in Proverbs Solomon warns the adulterer about the fury of a jealous husband (Prov. 6:34).

Moral sin is progressive. You may start out losing interest in your own wife. Then, you notice another woman's beauty. Then, you embrace her beauty in your heart and mind and take the step that you vowed you never would: you step out.

Commenting on the progression of sin, Steve Gallagher wrote,

> Left to himself, the sinner hurls himself into sin. Burning with an intense flame of lust, he finds himself no longer able to restrain himself. Deeper and deeper he sinks into the foul cesspool of depravity. Nothing is too gross, shameful, or forbidden. The cup of iniquity is now full. Sin has been given complete reign over the man's mind. (At the Altar of Sexual Idolatry [Dry Ridge, KY: Pure Life Ministries, 2000], p. 31)

"The evil deeds of a wicked man ensnare him; the cords of his sin hold him fast" (v. 22).

My friend's horse had to listen to the voice of his master and quit asserting his own will. We do too. We are not much different from that horse. Husbands, listen to the voice of your master, God, and appreciate your wife's beauty. Wives, listen to the voice of your master, God. During the dating years, you delighted in your husband's attention to your beauty, and you still can. You can even encourage it. Your steps to the altar began with physical attention and allure. You can still delight in each other and keep each other from unholy snares.

THE SEDUCTIVE WOMAN

At the window of my house, I looked out through the lattice. I saw among the simple, I noticed among the young men, a youth

who lacked judgment. He was going down the street near her
corner, walking along in the direction of her house at twilight, as
the day was fading, as the dark of night set in. Then out came a
woman to meet him.

—Proverbs 7:6–10a

This passage introduces a story of a young man who is led inch by inch,
inducement by inducement, into an apparent dreamworld, a world of fantasy,
love, and sensuality, but also into a world that is really death and decay.

Proverbs 7 begins with an admonition from Solomon to his son: "My
son, keep my words and store up my commands within you. Keep my
commands and you will live . . . they will keep you from the adulteress, from
the wayward wife with her seductive words" (Prov. 7:1–2a; 5).

The seductive woman actually uses more than just words in her arsenal
to appeal to young men. She uses an appeal to eyesight. She is dressed like a
prostitute, alluringly attired and pleasing to the eyes (Prov. 7:10). She appeals
to touch. Verse 13 says she takes hold of him. She appeals to his hearing.
She speaks to him, and she uses persuasive words and smooth talk (Prov.
7:13 and 21). She appeals to his sense of smell by perfuming her bed (Prov.
7:17). Finally, the seductive woman appeals to his sense of taste. She kisses
him and speaks of drinking deeply of love (Prov. 7:13 and 18).

The seductive woman uses all five of a man's senses against him! How
can a man possibly resist this woman's advances when her arsenal of weapons
attacks every one of his senses: his sight, touch, hearing, smell, and taste?
The poor guy doesn't stand a chance unless he keeps the words of wisdom
passed on to him from his father. Unless he uses this wisdom to resist her,
he is no better off than an ox trudging along to the slaughter (Prov. 7:22).

There is another way of looking at the seductive woman's tactics. She
uses shock with her provocative clothing. Caught in the allure of her looks,
the young man is further shocked into her orbit with her sensuous kiss.
She uses celebration ("I have fellowship offerings at home!") and flattery
("I looked for you and have found you!"). Of all the men in the world, she
has eyes only for you! The seductive woman uses the sensuous appeal of her
meticulously prepared private quarters. Finally, she offers reassurance: "It
is going to be ok, my husband is not at home" (Derek Kidner, "Proverbs"
Tyndale [Downer's Grove, IL: InterVarsity Press, 1979], p. 75).

Even a guy who wants to maintain his purity and save himself for his
wife doesn't stand a chance against such a woman if his guard is down. It is
going to take everything he has to resist her. It will take the unified effort

of heart, eyes, and body to resist her. A man's successful defense relies on doing the following:

1. Keeping his heart and mind away from her. Verse 25a says, "Do not let your heart turn to her ways." Another verse says, "Above all else, guard your heart, for it is the wellspring of life" (4:23). Moral purity begins in the heart.
2. Keeping his body away from her. "Do not . . . stray into her paths" (7:25b). Impure thoughts combined with close physical proximity stokes the fires of passion. Remember what Joseph did when this was happening to him!
3. Keeping his eyes focused past her . . . to the *end*. What if you give in to her? Focus your eyes beyond the temporary pleasure to the tragic consequences: "Her house is a highway to the grave, leading down to the chambers of death" (7:27).

Men, when the beauty and allure of an enticing woman beckons us, we must remember that moral purity is our responsibility. If we want our girlfriends to wait for us and our wives to be true to us, we must exercise the same moral restraint we expect of them. To do that we must focus on the wisdom of God that can keep us "from the wayward wife" and keep us in the secure relationship of our wives.

ANNIVERSARY

A wife of noble character is her husband's crown, but a disgraceful wife is like decay in his bones.

—Proverbs 12:4

March 20 is an important day in our household. That is our anniversary. In memory of that date, I could have entitled this, "See, I remembered." I could have entitled it, "The happiest day of my life." That would not be an exaggeration.

Cheryl and I walked the aisle on March 20, 1982. It was a happy day. Every anniversary is a happy day because every year we celebrate it as a positive reminder that our marriage is moving in the direction God wants it to.

Marriage is God's idea. Man didn't think to himself, "We have a lot of social systems in place right now—schools, community, sports programs, and 4-H. But something is missing. What we need is . . . well, something that binds a man and woman together for life. Something that so intertwines their lives that they couldn't or wouldn't think about ending it. Something that creates such a warm environment that it would provide the ideal place for raising children. What could that be? Hey, let's invent marriage!"

There are social scientists who believe that the existence of marriage is a purely human construct; that sometime back in the annals of history, man and woman, through social engineering and experimentation, happened upon marriage. They explain the origination of marriage in completely human terms. Some of them see the dissolution of a marriage as nothing more than the dissolution of any social contract, such as pulling your child off the community baseball team because he decides he doesn't like the game.

There is more to marriage than that. Genesis 2 says that God looked at the man he created and saw him alone in the Garden. God said, "It is not good for the man to be alone. I will make a helper suitable for him." It was then that God created Eve. However, that does not mean that the woman was an afterthought. From the very beginning, God made it clear that a man and woman together was his plan. I think the idea in this verse is not that God just got the idea because he saw the man was alone. I think it means that God said, "Now is the time to complete my plan. Man has been alone long enough to realize what a blessing a wife will be to his life."

So God made Eve for Adam.

Adam did perceive Eve to be a blessing. Adam said, "She is now bone of my bones and flesh of my flesh." God looked at this union and said, "A man will leave his father and mother and be united to his wife, and they will become one flesh."

One flesh. They are no longer two, but one. Over time a husband and wife grow closer together in their thoughts, their attitudes, and their desires. Ideally, as children enter the union, the husband and wife are drawn even closer together. They now share the concerns for their children as well as their health, their spiritual life, their future. This is just how God planned it.

Every time an anniversary rolls around for your marriage, you have a fresh cause for celebration. You have shown to yourselves and the world that in your union God is still at work. If, after the usual stresses and strains of marriage, you are *still* together after one year, twenty-five years, and fifty years, remember that day and thank God for it.

A GOOD WIFE

He who finds a wife finds what is good and receives favor from the Lord.

—Proverbs 18:22

If you have a wife who loves you, seeks your best interests and cares for you, you know the truth of this proverb. It doesn't have to be explained. Your life is deeply enriched because of the presence of this woman who loves you, your wife. "He who finds a wife finds what is good and receives favor from the Lord."

As a kid, I remember listening to the words of a Charley Pride song that my dad played in our house:

Whenever I chance to meet, some old friends on the street, They wonder how does a man get to be this way. I've always got a smiling face, at anytime and anyplace, And every time they ask me why I just smile and say:

(Chorus)

You've got to kiss an angel good morning, And let her know you think about her when you're gone. Kiss an angel good morning, And love her like the devil when you get back home.

Well, people may try to guess, the secret of our happiness, But some of them never learn that it's a simple thing. The secret that I'm speaking of, is a woman and a man in love, And the answer is in this song that I always sing.

(Chorus)

That song, "Kiss an Angel Good Morning," could be Charley's commentary on this verse from Proverbs, "He who finds a wife finds what is good and receives favor from the Lord."

The Bible proclaims marriage to be a blessing. Sure, there are stories of husbands and wives who don't function as they should and, their home lives are not always satisfying. Think of David. But that is not how God wants it.

God plans for marriage to be fulfilling, satisfying, and uplifting. "The Lord God said, 'It is not good for the man to be alone. I will make a helper suitable for him'" (Gen. 2:18). He did. He made Eve, a wife for Adam. So long as they focused on each other and met the needs of their partner, things went smoothly for Adam and Eve. It was only after they selfishly ate of the forbidden fruit that their attention began to focus on themselves and their needs. When that happened, well, we know what happens when husbands and wives are selfish. Things don't go the way they should.

A husband who can say, "He who finds a wife finds what is good and receives favor from the Lord" is a husband who thinks about his wife, loves her, and knows the blessing she is to his life. He appreciates her. He knows, as the Sage wrote in yet another proverb, that a good wife "is from the Lord" (Prov. 19:14).

To all of you men who have been blessed by God with a good wife, appreciate her. Let her know it. Let her be the angel you greet with joy first thing in the morning and the last thing at night. If she brings gladness into your life, reflect some of that gladness back to her. Let her know that in her you have found something good.

With this little tribute to wives, let me add a "thank you" to my wife Cheryl.

A WIFE FROM THE LORD

> Houses and wealth are inherited from parents, but a prudent wife
> is from the Lord.
>
> —Proverbs 19:14

Houses and wealth have value. Thirty years is the typical time to pay for a house. Accumulating enough wealth to retire comfortably takes a lifetime. Houses and wealth are objects of great value! Fortunate is the person who inherits these from his parents and can enjoy financial ease and peace earlier in life.

We place great stock in houses and wealth. Ask someone what it would take for them to regard their lives as a success and many people will answer, "Oh, if I can get my dream house" or "To have enough money to live comfortably and travel." Houses and wealth provide comfort and status.

We evaluate ourselves and others on the basis of houses, cars, clothing, and savings accounts.

However, the value of houses and wealth is limited. Though we work forty years for them or inherit them from the lifelong labor of our parents, they are still only material items. Houses will deteriorate and wealth can slip through our fingers. If we don't spend our money, someone will be happy to after we are gone.

The Sage recognizes the value of houses and wealth, and he gives credit to parents who pass them on to their children. But he recognizes one blessing that comes directly from God: a prudent wife.

Prudent means wise, but it is not wise or smart in the sense of making all A's in school or doing a crossword puzzle without having to look in the dictionary. Wisdom in Proverbs has to do with skill in relationships. Wisdom means knowing when and how to encourage, rebuke, soothe, or scold. To be wise in a relationship means not demeaning people, mocking them, or hurting their feelings. Wisdom means knowing how to communicate value, love, and dignity to others. Wisdom also means caring about others in your life and working to serve their needs.

A prudent wife is one who loves her husband, walks with him in life, and seeks to build a lifelong bond. She is concerned about his physical needs and encourages his success in the workplace. Being a prudent wife and being concerned about her husband does not mean she doesn't have interests or skills of her own. Certainly, the portrait of the wise woman in Proverbs 31 is of a woman who is emotionally secure and socially skilled. But even in this picture, her energy is devoted to the care and nurture of her family.

A prudent wife, one who forgoes many of her own interests to consider the needs of her husband and children first, is a gift from God. She can't be passed on like a house or a bank account. She is generally raised and nurtured in a believing home. She is taught by her parents to worship God. Love for the Lord is planted in her heart at an early age and blossoms into personal faith and spiritual living. She is a blessing to the lives of those around her. A discerning young man recognizes her inestimable qualities and seeks to capture her heart. Fortunate is the young man who does!

"A prudent wife is from the Lord" means that God is the source of the blessing of this wonderful woman. It also means that the husband must always recognize and honor her great value. "Nothing on earth more clearly reveals the holiness and mercy of God than she does" (Dan Allender and Tremper Longman, Intimate Allies [Wheaton, IL: Tyndale, 1995], p. 35). The value of houses and wealth pale alongside the blessing of the prudent wife. Keep material pursuits in proper perspective. Give all the energy you can to nurturing your relationship with your prudent wife, and express appreciation to her for all she means to you.

RIGHT AND JUST

To do what is right and just is more acceptable to the Lord than sacrifice.

—Proverbs 21:3

Cheryl and I awoke one Saturday morning to the sound of voices in our living room, something that surprised us since we didn't have kids or company. I rushed into the living room to find my brother Jim from Texas and a friend Chuck from Tennessee. Cheryl and I were living in Florida. My brother and friend thought it would be a good idea for us all to get together again. So they drove all night to visit us in Florida, unannounced. "What are you guys doing here?" I asked. "Oh, we just wanted to come and say 'Hi,'" they replied.

Jim and Chuck stayed for several days. It was like old times; target practicing, playing sports, and visiting. Sunday night after church a group of us had pizza. Afterward, Chuck asked, "How about some basketball?" As I was walking out of the house, I asked Cheryl, "Do you mind?" She smiled. I saw her mom smile, as well. They had given me their blessing to go do my guy thing.

Cheryl was a good sport that weekend. We were three twenty-something guys revisiting our teen years. It's fine to be a teenager when you are a teenager. It's even okay to do sometimes when you are a bit older. But there is a time to grow up and take a mature view of things. I hope I have done that. Cheryl was gracious and patient during the time it took for me to mature as a husband.

Some guys never grow up. They marry and take on adult responsibilities but never fully assume them. They dump the raising of the children on their wife. They take off on hunting or sports trips without even checking the schedule with their wife or without even considering if it is appropriate for them to go at the time. They get short and sarcastic if their wives say, "Hey, wait a minute, how about some help around here with the house, the kids, and the yard!" They don't want their lifestyles crimped by the relational needs and demands that being a good husband and responsible father require. In short, they never grow up and take a mature view of their lives, their family, or the world.

When a guy like this realizes he has crossed the line, he may give his wife some flowers, a card, and an apology, thinking that will somehow make everything right. But, if he looks carefully, he can see the hurt in her eyes. "What's the matter, don't you like the flowers?"

"Oh, of course I do. But I would rather have your time, your respect, your consideration, and your love. Help me. Work with me. Take the kids for an afternoon so I can rest."

"To do what is right and just is more acceptable to the Lord than sacrifice." God prefers our hearts, our love, our obedience, and our ethics over any act of worship that is meant more to appease his anger than to glorify his greatness (See Proverbs 15:8). I don't think that verse needs to be explained to a wife who has just been handed a beautiful bouquet but who really wants to know that her husband loves her and cherishes her in his life. Such a husband communicates that love, occasionally with roses but always with kindness, devotion, and his presence. That is right and just. It is also the recipe for a marriage that not only weathers the storms of life but actually rises above them.

HONESTY AND A KISS

An honest answer is like a kiss on the lips.
—Proverbs 24:26

I want to argue with that proverb. "I do appreciate honesty, and I know God demands honesty from people. I know that honesty is crucial in all relationships, especially in marriage. But an expression of intimacy like a kiss, between a loving husband and wife, is in a category all its own."

In fairness to the Sage and his social and cultural era, a kiss had a larger function than just expressing affection between a husband and wife. A kiss was a means of offering a greeting or of expressing friendship, reconciliation, and loyalty between all family members, friends, and even of citizens to a ruler (Bruce Waltke, The Book of Proverbs: New International Commentary on the Old Testament [Grand Rapids: Eerdmans Publishing Co., 2005], 2:292–93). In some ways a kiss was comparable to our practice of shaking hands, a means of greeting and expressing friendship. I like our custom of reserving the kiss to the more intimate relationships, like between husband and wife.

However, the real issue in this proverb is not the kiss but the honesty of one's conversation. "An honest answer is like a kiss on the lips." Assuming the kiss on the lips to be a sweet experience, the Sage says that for a person of integrity and character, honesty is that sweet. Listen to another passage from Proverbs about honesty:

> Listen, for I have worthy things to say; I open my lips to speak what is right. My mouth speaks what is true, for my lips detest wickedness. All the words of my mouth are just; none of them is crooked or perverse. To the discerning all of them are right; they are faultless to those who have knowledge. (Prov. 8:6–9)

Wisdom personified is speaking here. Wisdom declares that the honest person can speak words that are not crooked or perverse because he has no insincere or selfish motives. Honest words come from a pure heart. Wisdom also declares that discerning people, those who have a godly perspective and character, can recognize truth and honesty.

People of high character who speak the truth and have a discerning spirit recognize purity and honesty in other people. They enjoy a sweetness of fellowship that the less honest, pure, and discerning cannot appreciate or understand. When people with pure hearts meet, there is a mutuality of openness and authenticity between them. There is no need to hide feelings, slant answers, or manipulate impressions. They express feelings and opinions with naturalness and transparency. They do not fret about what the other person will think because their goal is to be faithful and true to what they are expressing. They know lesser characters may take offense at the honesty and scurry away, but larger and grander souls will gravitate toward such faithful communication. A friendship formed between honest people will be deep, real, and faithful.

Such honesty is needed in all relationships, whether in business, church, politics, or friendship. Such honesty is essential in marriage. "An honest answer is like a kiss on the lips." Such honesty is a vital ingredient to the level of trust that is necessary for a husband and wife to walk together for fifty years. The sweetness of their kisses can only endure if it is in the context of the sweetness of transparency and trust. Listen to the advice of a marriage counselor:

When honesty and cooperation exist in a marriage, you have a couple who is willing to share and to build together. They do not need to be secretive or private. Neither wishes to lie and shade the truth to protect the spouse. When you build your marriage on trust, you experience a joyful willingness to share all personal feelings with the one you have chosen for a life partner. (Willard F. Harley, Jr., His Needs, Her Needs: Building an Affair-Proof Marriage [Grand Rapids: Fleming H. Revell, 1986], p. 102)

Kissing may still be in a category by itself, but it must share attention with honesty. If you want your marriage to be a great one, give as much attention to the purity of your heart as to the sweetness of your affection.

Mom, Dad, And The Kids

LISTEN, MY SON

Listen, my son, to your father's instruction and do not forsake your mother's teaching.

—Proverbs 1:8

Over twenty times Solomon writes "my son" followed by an exhortation such as, "Listen, my son" or "My son, do not forget." Solomon is offering some concrete instruction to bolster his son's insight and moral conditioning. There is a great emphasis in Proverbs for a son or daughter to listen to what Solomon has to say. His advice is right in line with what Christian parents today tell their kids. He emphasizes that children need to listen to their moms and dads and to apply the lessons being taught about love, marriage, hard work, and honesty.

There is an important lesson for the parents here as well. It is as critical for the parents to teach as it is for the children to listen. Our kids can't listen and they can't learn if we are not actively instructing them. I think we parents make two grave mistakes when it comes to teaching lessons of life to our children.

First of all, we think they will pick up the important lessons from us by mere observation. Many lessons they will. "More is caught than taught" is often true but, not always. They may catch our behavior, but what about the thinking process behind our behavior? My children were not there when I picked their mother to be my wife. Why did I choose her? Was I attracted to her looks? Was I more attracted to her values and morals? Did I know before we married that she really wanted to be a wife and mother? The answer is yes to all these questions. But my kids can't know that apart from my telling them. In fact, I have told them many times. I want them to know the critical issues involved in selecting a mate for life, for choosing moral behavior, for working hard. These things are too important to be left to chance! They must be taught. By teaching them, we equip them to make wiser choices than they could make on their own.

Secondly, we think we can expect obedient behavior "because we say so." That is parental authority, and it works great when the kids are little. They wouldn't understand detailed explanations anyway. But what about when they grow older and begin making decisions on their own? Or when they are away from us? What is it that internalizes our values into their hearts? There comes a time when "because we say so" must give way to "this is why I say this" or "this is why we want you to do this." As they mature, we need to let them know the reasons we expect certain behavior. Once they know and understand and it gets into their hearts, it belongs to them.

"Bobby" is an example of a child who was drilled with "because I say so" but was never schooled in the reasons. Bobby's crowd began drinking. His mother "freaked out" and assumed an authoritarian posture. "If I catch you drinking and driving, I'll make your life miserable!" Mom was acting for the good of the boy. She was the parent and had the right to insist on more mature behavior from her son. But, her lessons failed to internalize in her son so that he could understand the reason for her concern. She never explained to him the dangers of drinking and how it could lead to further irresponsible behavior, loss of control, and even an accident or death. Bobby thought he was old enough to make his own choices. One night he drank too much. Fearing that his mother would find out, he decided not to call her. He tried driving home on his own but didn't make it. The mother and young child he hit were severely injured (Phil McGraw, Family First [New York: Free Press, 2005], p. 167).

Contrast this story with another teenage boy whose dad did school him on the reasons for not drinking. He still experimented. He drove home from one teen party with a beer in his hand, but the wisdom of his parents' counsel worked on his conscience. Thinking how it would hurt his mom and dad to see him with that, the boy opened the window and threw out the beer. Sure, he littered, but he did honor his dad's instruction. "Listen, my son."

PARENTING HERITAGE

Listen, my sons, to a father's instruction; pay attention, and gain understanding. I give you sound learning, so do not forsake my teaching. When I was a boy in my father's house, still tender, and an only child of my mother, he taught me and said, "Lay hold of my words with all your heart; keep my commands and you will live."

—Proverbs 4:1–4

We become what we were raised to be. Much of the process is unconscious. It happens naturally as we grow up and go about life.

I like baseball and hunting. When I was just a boy, even before I was old enough to carry a gun myself, I went hunting with my dad, grandpa, and a couple of uncles. It was just something our family did. It was the same with baseball. My grandfather bought me one of my first baseball gloves. I used to go to his house to watch ball games. My dad coached my brothers and me for years. Little by little, without fanfare or awareness, I became an enthusiast for the woods and the ballpark. I have now passed on that same enthusiasm to my own kids.

Our parenting style is something we were developing when we were still little kids. We didn't think about it, we didn't reflect on it, and we didn't consciously develop it. We became the parents we are today by the parenting style we were raised under when we were two years old, five years old, thirteen years old, and eighteen years old. We were parented to be parents.

Such a reality is at the same time both frightening and exciting. It is frightening because if the parenting style we were raised under was not sound, our parenting style won't be either. If our parents were neglectful or abusive, there is a good chance we will treat our kids in the same way. On the other hand, if our parents' style was healthy, then our style likely will be as well. If we were loved and nurtured, we will tend to practice that same kind of care toward our own children.

In Proverbs 4:1–4, when Solomon is passing on instruction to his son, he draws from his own experience as a boy and the parenting care he received from his mom and dad. When he refers to himself as tender and the only child of his mother, you can picture Bathsheba's gentle care for him. When he refers to being a boy when his father taught him, you can see David sitting at the dinner table, saying, "Son," and then passing on some words of fatherly care and advice. Now, as an adult, Solomon draws from that experience and practices the same level of care with his own son.

When we become adults, we generally parent like our parents, but we don't have to be locked into a certain pattern. If our parents had an unhealthy style, we don't have to parent as they did, and we don't have to engage our kids the way our parents did us. As adults, we can reflect. We can think and say, "You know, I like the way my parents handled some situations but not the way they handled others." We can decide to be more patient, compassionate or involved than we perceive our parents to have been.

Dr. Phil McGraw says there are two common ways of reflecting the parenting style of our parents. One, we parent our own children just the way they parented us. If they hollered at the kids for any infraction, then we probably will as well. The second response is to react against the way our parents raised us. If we regard our parents as having been too strict, we may become overly lenient (Family First, p. 67). I think the important thing to realize is this . . . we have a choice in the kind of parents we will be. With proper reflection, dependence upon the Word, prayer, and continued mentoring from and accountability to older Christian parents with a proven track record in parenting, we can incorporate the very best of our parents' style into our own approach to parenting. We can enhance our parenting legacy with the instruction of our parents and the ongoing instruction we can receive from other Christian people God puts in our lives.

WHAT A FATHER DOES

When I was a boy in my father's house, still tender, and an only child of my mother, he taught me and said, "Lay hold of my words with all your heart; keep my commands and you will live."
—Proverbs 4:3–4

It was not by accident that Solomon became the wisest man in the world. Solomon prayed for wisdom (1 Kings 3:7–9). Because he prayed, God gave Solomon wisdom as a gift (1 Kings 3:12; 4:29). Solomon was also blessed to have a dad who taught him (Prov. 4:3–9).

Solomon was still a boy, tender, young, and impressionable, when his dad taught him. "Lay hold of my words," his father said. In other words, "grab them! Keep my commands and live." Life in wisdom literature is not necessarily a long life, but quality of life (Prov. 19:23, 22:4), a good life.

Solomon's dad, David, continued his admonition to his son in following verses. "Get wisdom, get understanding," he told Solomon (Prov. 4:5). Wisdom is skill in living. David is teaching Solomon, "Learn about life."

David tells his son, "Wisdom is supreme, therefore get wisdom" (Prov. 4:7). Wisdom is more than knowledge. A person can have knowledge about a variety of things, even good things, but still be empty. Wisdom's focus is not about the accumulation of knowledge but of relationships. Wisdom has to do with relationship with God, other people, and self. The relationship we have with ourselves is our character. A person of wisdom is spiritual, exercising discipline, maturity, and morality.

This describes the wise person in Proverbs. So what is the fool? The fool is one who fails in these areas. He may go to church, but he doesn't pray, "Lord, how do I live to please you?" The fool hates knowledge so he does not fear the Lord and obey him (Prov. 1:29–30). His relationship with God is shallow. His relationships with others are weak. The fool is selfish, so he doesn't know how to serve in relationships or how to be a loyal friend. Finally, the fool's relationship with himself is dishonest. The fool consistently makes decisions that lack integrity, morals, and discipline. It is not that he or she makes mistakes; we all do. But for a fool, his lack of character is a way of life.

How important is wisdom in your relationship with God, with others, or with yourself? David tells his son, "Wisdom is supreme; therefore, get wisdom. Though it cost all you have, get understanding" (v.7). Wisdom is worth more than all you have. So "embrace her" (v. 8). Embrace wisdom. This is a word to describe how a loving husband treats his wife — he embraces her. It is a word of love and romance. There are physical and emotional dimensions to embracing. Physically it is a hug; emotionally or spiritually, it means to be devoted to. David uses this word to his son about wisdom: "Embrace her, love her."

Solomon is a man now, the king. He is remembering back to when he was a tender little boy. He remembers his dad saying, "Love wisdom, son. Be devoted to it."

I am impressed with what David did not teach his son. He didn't say, "Get a good job and make a lot of money." If you have wisdom, you will get a job. David didn't tell his son to be popular. Some parents want their kids to be popular so much that they buy the alcohol for their kids' parties. These parents are actually sabotaging their kids' chance of becoming wise. David didn't teach Solomon to pursue worldly attainments. "Get wisdom, son. You won't be everybody's friend, but the friends you have will be real. You'll have your relationship with God. And you can know that your character is impeccable."

Those are the things a father does. He orients his children to what is important. He models them in his own life, and he actively teaches the principles and substance of wisdom: relationship with God, with others, with self. Thank you, fathers, for what you do.

STRAIGHT PATHS

Listen, my son, accept what I say, and the years of your life will be many. I guide you in the way of wisdom and lead you along straight paths. When you walk, your steps will not be hampered; when you run, you will not stumble.

—Proverbs 4:10–12

I remember watching two teenage boys trying to build a fence. Their father had given them the assignment, but he didn't demonstrate how to perform the task. The boys were left on their own to supervise themselves and complete the work.

After striking a line so the fence would be straight, the boys had to dig the holes, insert the posts and nail the cross rails. Not an easy job. What little the boys did accomplish was not sturdy. The interest of the boys soon waned and they abandoned their tools and went inside. For several weeks the tools remained in the dirt where the boys let them fall.

This job was a good assignment for the boys. It could have taught them to appreciate hard work. They could have learned the proper use of tools. They could have experienced the joy of completing a job. But they didn't. Instead, discouragement and frustration set in, and they quit.

I related this story to an older friend of mine, Marion Phillips. Marion said, "The dad tried to teach the boys a work ethic and craftsmanship. He wanted them to learn how to use their hands. His mistake was turning the job over to the boys and leaving them unsupervised. He needed to work with them, explaining what to do and showing them how to do it. If you don't explain, show, and help, they won't know how to build the fence. Other valuable lessons will be lost as well."

Explain the task. Show them how to do it. Help them complete the job.

Marion's advice has a broader application than just teaching boys how to build a fence. It applies to helping our children build a life, teaching them the way of wisdom and straight paths.

I remember a professor telling our class that one of the best ways to enter into a conversation with our children is through doing things with them. The professor was jogging with his preteen daughter. They stopped for a rest. As he was lying on the ground chewing on a blade of grass, his daughter said, "Dad, some of the kids at school use bad words." Silence. Dad said nothing, not knowing what to say. "I say them, too, sometimes. But I know I shouldn't." An open door. A door for Dad to enter and lovingly share his values and impart his wisdom. No lectures, no heavy load of information, just a father getting into the business of life with his daughter, jogging, resting, listening. She was the one who opened up and invited Dad into her world.

Marion was right. We can't just tell our kids what to do. We need to explain, to show and to help them, whether it is a backyard project or living life with integrity. In this way, over the course of years, parental insight and adult wisdom are passed to the next generation, a generation that will be able to walk better because they can see the straight paths and have the desire to walk them.

Solomon promises long life for such a wise, young person. Does he literally mean more years? He probably means better years. "When you walk, your steps will not be hampered." The twenty-year-old with the wisdom beyond his years will more fully enjoy the blessings of this life because he has avoided many of the pitfalls that devastate less astute lives. So, parents, take the plunge, get in there with your kids and show them the business of life.

TEACH THE CHILDREN

Hold on to instruction, do no let it go; guard it well, for it is your life.

—Proverbs 4:13

"Love the Lord your God with all your heart and with all your soul and with all your strength. These commandments that I give you today are to be upon your hearts. Impress them on your children. Talk about them when you sit at home and when you walk along the road, when you lie down and when you get up. Tie them as symbols on your hands and bind them on your foreheads. Write them on the doorframes of your houses and on your gates" (Deut. 6:5–9).

Parents, teach your children. You can't leave it up to other teachers or schools or preachers or church. Certainly don't leave it up to the TV or your children's peer group! Parents are the primary teachers of their children.

Moses, the author of this passage, was not so concerned about teaching reading, writing, and math skills. He was concerned with parents passing on the history of God's dealing with their ancestors and the ethical and religious instruction of God.

Every avenue of instruction is to be explored and used. Use opportunities for conversation in the morning and in the evening, while sitting around or while traveling. Use the written word, putting messages or notes where they will be read and memorized by the children. Teach the children in any way you can, impressing upon them the important truths of our faith!

Important things happen when children are taught by the parents when they are young. One, they develop interest in what the parents are interested in. Children very naturally want to imitate their mom and dad. Whatever mom and dad give time and attention to, the children often do as well. It is no accident that my children like seafood. Their mom and I do! We introduced them to shrimp and oysters before they could even talk. Before they could talk, we introduced them to spiritual things as well. Their mom and I hope and pray that they will maintain a lifelong interest in this area as a result.

Secondly, having conversations with your children about important matters of faith, history, and God creates a powerful inner voice within them. Everyone engages in positive or negative self-talk. Children who perform poorly often have an internal conversation with themselves that is negative: "I can't, no one likes me, or I'm not good at that." On the other hand, children with positive self-talk, such as, "I can," tend to perform at a higher level in school and other activities. It wasn't a concern for Moses that children do well in sports because of their self-talk. But it was a concern of his that our kids do well living out the demands of discipleship. Teaching and conversing with them about important matters of faith is grist for the mill of their "inner voice"—their thinking and living.

Thirdly, as the children grow, they begin to develop competence in their knowledge of God's Word and the ability to apply it to life. We give them the concepts. We reinforce those concepts during dinner-table talks and conversations in the car on the way to ball games. We introduce new terms, such as "redemption" and "penitence," and stimulate their thinking yet more. Later, when they are faced with temptations from their peers or a friend gets in trouble with the law, their little world is shaken. But their internal dialogue of spiritual things, their knowledge of the Word, their commitment to live for God, keeps them rooted. They are able to "hold on to instruction (and) . . . guard it well." Their world may shake around them, but they can hold steady and secure inside. They are able to faithfully love their Lord with all their heart because their parents took the time and effort to plant and water that seed of trust over many years.

A PARENT'S TRAINING

> My son, keep your father's commands and do not forsake your mother's teaching. Bind them upon your heart forever; fasten them around your neck. When you walk, they will guide you; when you sleep, they will watch over you; when you awake, they will speak to you.
>
> —Proverbs 6:20–22

Have you ever thought that what our children will be someday they are in the process of becoming right now? That is a powerful thought! "All your children will ever be, they are now becoming . . . What you do with them today, when they are two, three, four, five, six or sixteen years of age, will determine what they will do at age twenty-four, thirty-four, or forty-four" (McGraw, Family First, p. 11). To drive this idea home Dr. Phil adds, "You are raising adults. Right now, they are under construction, like a new house being built from the ground up."

We parents frequently say, "We are raising our kids." We all know what we mean by that. We are cooking meals, doing laundry, going to school and sports programs, helping with homework, and practicing discipline, both instructive and corrective. But to say, "We are raising our kids" is to just look at the present and assess our work in the immediate. Do we see the long-term effect of going to a sports program, helping with homework, or punishing disobedience? We are raising adults! The goal of all of our daily activities with our children is not just to take up time with them; it is to shape their character, give them direction, and forge their destiny.

No wonder Solomon says, "My son, keep your father's commands and do not forsake your mother's teaching."

What we as parents do in our daily interactions with our children plants deep within them the compost from which will spring their future thoughts, decisions, and actions. The time spent at ball games becomes something more than an opportunity to cheer a victory; it demonstrates our support of their interests. The time spent on homework is more than helping them learn how to get the right answers; it is instilling self-discipline. The time spent on disciplining them—either instructing them or correcting them—is more than just trying to get them to behave so we won't be embarrassed by their behavior; it is "bending the twig" to grow in a healthy direction for life.

"My son, keep your father's commands and do not forsake your mother's teaching." A young man or woman keeping the father's and mother's instructions presupposes that dad and mom have been teaching at every moment and at every opportunity! It is time-consuming and can be demanding, but it is so worth the effort for the parents and the children! Done well, this teaching will take root in our children's hearts and will guide them through a wise and happy life. Solomon even says in the next two verses, "For these commands are a lamp, this teaching is a light, and the corrections of discipline are the way to life, keeping you from the immoral woman." Solomon's words are just as true for a daughter: proper training and words of wisdom implanted in her heart by her parents will keep her from an immoral man.

"All your children will ever be, they are now becoming . . . You are raising adults. Right now, they are under construction, like a new house being built from the ground up."

That little boy swinging the baseball bat? That little girl trying to sink a basket? They won't be little for long. Enjoy your time with them! Soak up every ball game, every school program, every question they ask. These are the golden opportunities of today for constructing the life that tomorrow will be an adult.

CAN I COME TO YOUR OFFICE?

A good man leaves an inheritance for his children's children.
—Proverbs 13:22

"Dad, can I come to your office?"

In Florida we lived in the shadow of the church building. Only a big, grassy yard separated our house from my office. It was safe for the kids, even when very little, to walk across the yard on their own. Cheryl would call me at the church office, the kids would get on and ask, "Dad, can I come to your office?" and I'd be on the lookout.

What was the attraction with my office? The desk. They would sit on my desk and ruffle the papers. Better yet, they liked to sit in my lap, pull out the top drawer of my desk, and rifle through everything.

I remember sometimes losing my patience. "Kids, I don't have time for this right now!" When they were finished, I would have White-Out, pencils, papers, and pens scattered all over the top of my desk! Can anyone blame me for not always being congenial about having my desk wrecked?

But at other times I remember thinking: "Enjoy this while you can. They won't always be sitting in your lap, content to just be with you. Let them play in the desk and make a mess. Someday you'll wish they could be around to do this again." On those days I'd just sit back in the chair and watch them have fun. Their having fun provided enjoyment for me. When it was over, I still had the mess to clean up, but it was worth it.

All three kids had their opportunities in my various offices. All three climbed around on the top of the desk, dug through the drawers, took over my chair, banged meaningless symbols and lines on the computer and demanded that it be printed and saved. All three in their early years thought my office was a fun place to be.

I'm glad they did. They're all older now, so sitting at my desk doesn't hold the same appeal to them as it once did. Other pursuits occupy their interests—baseball, softball, volleyball, soccer, debating. But I'm glad of one thing—they still want me around. Perhaps it is because I used to let them sit in my lap and mess up my desk. I'm sure they don't remember all the office and desk episodes, but the psychological and spiritual conditioning from those experiences are still embedded within them. The bonding and laughter is still with them. At game time they want their mom and me there.

Having small children is time-consuming and demanding. But is there anything more important for parents to do than to meet those time demands? Time is the stuff of life. Time with family, your children, friends. Whatever sermon, letter or bulletin article I was working on, when a little voice on the other end of the line asked, "Dad, can I come to your office," still got written. The work got done, I got paid, and the kids have grown older. Perhaps all I would change are the times I said, "No, not today."

Your kids want nothing more from you today than your time. They don't want your money, not really. They might enjoy the piece of candy your money can buy. But what they really want is you, whether it is playing

Candy Land, Mouse Trap, or Go Fish. Your kids want you, whether it is messing up your desk or sitting in your lap before they doze off to sleep. Don't disappoint them. Don't disappoint yourself.

God's greatest gift to you and your spouse are those children. Love and cherish every moment you spend together. Savor them. The time you enjoy in each other's company is the greatest inheritance you can leave your kids, and it is one they will pass on to your grandchildren. A good man leaves an inheritance of himself for his children and for their children to follow.

GOALS

The path of life leads upward for the wise.
—Proverbs 15:24

Most parents have goals for their kids. That is good; but until we plant our desires for our kids within their own hearts, so these desires become their own, our plans for our kids are empty. It is not enough that we want our children to be good students, to be polite and respectful, to be sober and abstain from alcohol or drugs, or that we want them to wait for marriage. No matter how seriously we desire these goals, they will not make a difference in the lives of our children until we somehow transfer them from our hearts to theirs.

Before we really talk about transferring goals to our kids, we need to consider our own personal goals. It will be hard for us to pass on important goals to our children if they don't see us pursuing worthy goals for ourselves. Do we have a goal to live responsibly within our income? Do we have a goal to spend time with our kids? Do we have a goal to feed our spiritual lives through personal study, prayer, and worship? If we don't have worthy goals that stretch us to higher levels of ethics and behavior, how inclined will our children be to accept the goals we have for them?

It is important that our goals for our children will be beneficial for them and will stretch them to be better people. We may have goals for our kids to be good athletes. I think that is worthy. Athletics creates friendships and builds community with teammates. Athletics gets our kids out of the house and away from the TV and has them running around a field or up and down a court. That promotes good health, and many kids are not getting enough physical activity. Athletics can help teach our children cooperation, leadership, and team spirit.

But is athletics the highest goal we have for them? You have probably seen, as I have, parents who place athletic accomplishment above any other goal for their children. Being a top athlete takes priority over worship, church youth activities, school work, summer jobs and even character development. But when high school graduation ends competitive sports for most kids, what is next? Many have not thought seriously about a college program, career track, or church involvement. When the final whistle sounds the end of their sports career, many of these young people are lost.

You have probably also seen athletics deteriorate to nothing more than winning or losing. "We have to win this game. We just have to! Our whole season hinges on this next throw, at-bat, or field-goal attempt. We have to win!" I want to ask, "Why?" Some of these kids are only eight years old. There are hundreds of games yet to unfold for them. Don't put so much pressure on them today that the joy of the game gets lost, and the guilt of missing the field goal or striking out lives with them longer than the sense of satisfaction for having tried.

What happens if our kids play their favorite sport all the way to high school, only to get a coach who doesn't like them or isn't fair and refuses to play them, no matter how talented they are? Hopefully you have built into the whole athletic process another set of goals more valuable than the sport itself: character development. If we don't have a goal to teach our children about patience, handling disappointment and defeat, practicing good sportsmanship even when the game is not going their way, and being positive even when you are being treated by your coach with disdain, then athletics as a goal has failed both us and our kids. Character development must be at the heart of youth sports, or youth sports will do more harm than good. Furthermore, if our kids are standout athletes who get to play all the time but have no character, they will be tough for anyone else to live with! An ungracious winner is even tougher to tolerate than an ungracious loser.

Athletic goals are best if they are used to help develop a more important purpose than simply winning, such as developing good character, Christian faith, and endurance in the face of disappointment. The higher purpose or goal looks beyond the scoreboard to the greater desired outcome—a young man or woman with moral substance, one whose path of life leads upward.

ENTITLEMENT AND EXEMPTION

A man's own folly ruins his life, yet his heart rages against the Lord.
—Proverbs 19:3

Old Western movies are generally rootin' tootin' features, but at least some of them have a good story line as well. Gunman's Walk is one example. In the movie Mr. Hackett, a rancher, has two sons, one a quiet and peaceful boy who tries to get his father's attention and the other, Ed, a loud would-be gunslinger.

Ed kills an Indian boy but is freed, compliments of a well-timed lying witness. Escaping a guilty charge enhances his sense of invincibility. He is the son of Lee Hackett. Nothing can corral his behavior, not even murder!

How can a boy develop such a hardened, uncaring attitude? How can he run roughshod over the lives of other people without even a twinge of conscience? Ed's dad has spoiled him. "My son can do no wrong!" The dad never actually used those words, but his actions seemed to say that. When the witness provided false testimony, the father said nothing. When the son extorted ten valuable horses from the ranch as payment for the lie, the father said nothing. When the son shot and wounded the lying witness, the father intervened to bribe the witness with even more reward to keep to his original story.

Dad could protect renegade Ed only so long. Ed staged a prison break, killing an unarmed deputy in the process. He then hopped on a horse and rode off across the countryside. While the sheriff raised a posse to apprehend the bad boy, the dad rode off after him as well. One more intervention on behalf of the boy?

My heart broke for the dad in the story. It was only a movie, but it had the flavor of real life. The dad tried to provide everything for his son that he could. The boy was raised in wealth and had everything he wanted. He was raised with entitlement, the belief that anything he wanted was his. Being a Hackett opened doors for this kid that were not opened for anyone else.

Entitlement led to something else that Ed Hackett just assumed he had . . . exemption, the freedom from any negative consequences due to his inappropriate behavior (Paul Warren and Frank Minirth discuss entitlement and exemption in Things That Go Bump in the Night, [Nashville, Thomas Nelson, 1992], p. 112 ff.). Ed thought he could do whatever he wanted without restraint. No one could reign him in; no one could tell him no, not even the sheriff. Furthermore, he suffered no negative consequences due to his aberrant behavior. He was exempt. After all, he was Ed Hackett.

But even Ed found out that entitlement and exemption go only so far. His dad pursued Ed into the countryside to confront him. Young Ed's behavior became so extreme that not even the dad could tolerate it anymore. The boy challenged his dad to see who was the faster draw. The dad was.

Gunman's Walk is not a pleasant story. It is a tough story about a father who failed and about a son who couldn't and wouldn't appreciate the blessings he had in life. Gunman's Walk is about two fools. "A man's own folly ruins his life." "Chasten your son while there is hope, and do not set your heart on his destruction" (Prov. 19:18 NKJV). Too late Mr. Hackett realized that what his son needed was less privilege and pampering and more tough love, instruction, and discipline at an early age. These attributes add up to wisdom, something God still honors today.

DISCIPLINE

Discipline your son, for in that there is hope; do not be a willing party to his death.

—Proverbs 19:18 (NIV)

Discipline your son while there is hope, and do not desire his death.

—Proverbs 19:18 (NASB)

There are two ways of reading and interpreting this verse, both of them valid. The Hebrew word kî, can mean for (casual) or it can mean while (temporal) (Dave Bland, Proverbs: College Press NIV Commentary [Joplin, MO: College Press Publishing, 2002], pp. 177–8).

"Discipline your son, for in that there is hope." This way of reading the verse says discipline plays an important role in shaping our children for life. Discipline is both instructional and corrective. Instructional discipline is when you teach your children to go to bed on time and not to talk back to you. Corrective discipline is when they disobey your rules and you have to punish them.

Children need to be taught the right way to behave and be corrected when they disobey. Describing his own experience with discipline, Solomon wrote, "When I was a boy in my father's house, still tender, and an only child of my mother, he (my father) taught me" (Prov. 4:3–4a). Discipline, instructional and corrective, molds a child's life to go in a positive direction.

"Discipline your son while there is hope." This second way of translating the verse puts the emphasis on the brief window of opportunity we have for this training and discipline. "You have to discipline your child, and there is only limited time to do it!"

When is the time to begin instructional and corrective discipline of children? As soon as they are old enough to understand what you are saying, they are ready to be disciplined. When you tell your children no and they challenge you ("What are you going to do about it!") or defy you ("Just watch me!"), they are ready for corrective discipline.

Parents administer corrective discipline in different ways. Some parents give a slap on the hand, some deny privileges, and others do time-out. Whatever form you choose to take, it must be administered immediately and firmly, and it must make an impression upon the child. The pain of disobedience must outweigh the pleasure of the disobedience. The children must learn that when you as the parent speak, you mean business. Rules are laid down and they are enforced. If you don't enforce the rules, even the minor ones, how will you enforce them when the kids are older and the issues are dating and driving the car? Respect is learned and earned in that window of opportunity when the children are young.

"Do not be a willing party to his death" or "Do not desire his death."

What parent would be a willing party to his child's death? What parent would desire his child's death? Like the previous part of the verse, this one has two possible meanings. One, it could refer to abusiveness; don't vent your anger or seek revenge to the extent that it results in the child's death.

The second view is that death here refers to failure in properly training the child, instilling inner discipline within his heart, and preparing him for a meaningful and productive life. Of the immoral life Proverbs says, "The dead are there" (Prov. 9:18). Concerning a life lived on the basis of irresponsible choices Proverbs says, "He who is contemptuous of his ways (or careless of his conduct [Prov. 19:16 NASB]) will die" (Prov. 19:16 NIV). "Folly is bound up in the heart of a child, but the rod of discipline will drive it far from him" (Prov. 22:15).

Every parent wants their children to grow up and have a "good life." That good life is found in living godly, wisely, and responsibly. That lifestyle is learned from parents who care enough to discipline.

HEART OF A CHILD

Even a child is known by his actions, by whether his conduct is
pure and right.

—Proverbs 20:11

Can you tell the heart of a child by his or her actions? Not always, because
even children can fool us. Generally though, conduct reveals content. Behavior
is telling. Jesus said, "For out of the heart come evil thoughts, murder,
adultery" (Matt. 15:19). The heart reveals conduct that is evil or pure.

Is that true even of a child? Does a child have the complexity of emotion
already in his or her heart: hate or love, cruelty or kindness, selfishness or
generosity? Do children have the capacity to feel gratitude and express
thankfulness? Can their hearts be so filled with love that they can respond
to a grandmother or grandfather with hugs and kisses? On the other hand,
can they be so self-centered that they don't say "thank you" or so disrespectful
that they slap adults?

I have seen young children open their hearts and reveal some amazingly
mature content. Even at a young age, children can extend themselves in
warm and caring ways. My son Wesley and I visited with a man whose wife
had to make a choice between him or her addiction to alcohol. She moved
a trailer to the back of the bar where she worked in a mountain town. She
left her husband so she could drink uninterrupted by family concerns.

She didn't just leave her husband. She also left her eleven-year-old son.
What kind of an impact do you think that would make on a child?

Can you imagine how this boy felt? He was hurting. But I remember
being impressed with how pure this child's heart still was. "I want my mom
back" was his grave concern.

This boy and Wesley found common ground in baseball. At the end
of our visit, he gave Wes a baseball bat. It was old, but it was all he had to
give to Wes to show the connection he made with him and how much he
appreciated that connection. Even in his hurt, his conduct was pure and
right. Somehow his father and maybe the mother, before she totally sold
herself to addiction, poured some good qualities into that little fella's heart.
"Even a child is known by his actions, by whether his conduct is pure and
right."

There is an interesting twist to this verse. It is possible that the statement,
"Even a child is known by his actions . . ." may not even refer to children;
it may refer to adults. The word "even" in the verse is the indication that

this statement is actually a comparison of adults to kids: "If even a child is known by his actions, by whether his conduct is pure and right, then an adult is known in the same way" (Bland, p. 184).

We can't really hide who we are or what we are all about, at least not for long. We may keep a lid on inner hostility for a while, but in time some circumstance will rip the lid off and venomous anger will pour forth. We may keep a screen up to hide our envy from view, but in time someone else's good fortune will rip that screen down and reveal our envy in all its ugliness. "If even a child is known by his actions, by whether his conduct is pure and right, then an adult is known in the same way."

The heart is the center of who we are and what we do. So keep it clean through confession and honesty, through worship of God, and through fellowship with other people of high character. Keep the heart pure and right, and actions that are pure and right will follow.

HERITAGE

Do not move an ancient boundary stone set up by your forefathers.
—Proverbs 22:28

I have a vague memory of boundary stones on our farm in Vermont and my two acres in Wyoming. Those markers set the limits of my property, but they also set the limits of the property bordering mine. We knew where our property and rights extended and ended. No questions. Like fences, boundary markers make good friends. They establish borders, determine rights, and provide order. If both sides of the boundary stones respect the markers, peace and order reigns.

So the Sage says, "Respect those markers!" Don't move them. You threaten a person's livelihood if you move a marker and deprive a landowner of his property. In ancient Israel and even for some in modern America, the land provides the food and the income for a family to survive. Deprive that family of income potential from the land, and you may bankrupt that family.

Those ancient boundary markers did more than guarantee property lines and rights; they provided a sense of continuity. In ancient Israel the property that God blessed each household with was passed on to succeeding generations. Fathers passed the land on to sons who then passed it on to their sons. Generations of a family would be raised on the same property, harvesting the same fields, wading the same creeks, and plucking fruit from the same trees. Those boundary markers provided a very important sense of stability for families, and that stability became an important element of the family's and society's heritage.

So if you moved an ancient boundary stone, you actually did more than disrupt the livelihood of that family, as important as that was. If you moved that stone, you "destroyed the social order and well-being of individuals in the community" (Bland, p. 206–07). You upset the order and jeopardized the heritage.

This verse is very important. Is there anything in our lives that provides a sense of heritage for us, a sense of continuity with our ancestors, a connection with our past? Is there something we can hold onto as a connection to grandma and grandpa, even great-grandma and grandpa? Fortunate are those who grow up on a farm and can say, "My dad and his mom were both born and raised on this farm. I'm the fourth generation in my family to farm this land." That is happening less and less.

In my own family, a construction business helped provide some of that heritage for me. I remember seeing tools of my dad's marked, "Baldwin and Baldwin." "Are these tools from the business you owned with grandpa?" I asked dad. "No," he said. "These are tools from the business your grandpa owned with your great-grandpa." At age thirteen, I was assembling some of the equipment my great-grandfather used back in 1930. That is heritage, a connection with my past, a boundary marker that establishes order, permanence, and stability.

My own children did not have the benefit of being raised on a farm or in a business that had been worked by four generations of my family. But I have found something that does serve as such a boundary marker for them, something that promotes heritage and stability. It is worship. My kids worship with their mother and me. At the same time but in other places, both sets of grandparents are worshiping. When a certain song is sung, I can lean over and whisper to one of my kids, "That was one of great-grandpa's favorite songs. When I was your age, I remember him leading this song all the time. He would sing it with his eyes closed, he knew it so well." And with that, I plant a boundary marker that will remain in place throughout the lifetime of my kids. It is a marker that connects them with grandparents, great-grandparents, and even great-great-grandparents, a marker that will weekly remind them of who they are, who they belong to, and how they are to live. Worship is an "ancient boundary stone set up by our fathers," so let's plant those markers deep into the hearts of our children and grandchildren.

MOTHERS ARE SPECIAL

May your father and mother be glad; may she who gave you birth rejoice!

—Proverbs 23:25

Why are mothers special? They give us life. God set in motion the procreative process many years ago, and even today God's plan needs godly women who are willing to pass life on to the next generation. Today, however, more and more women are choosing to forego motherhood for a variety of personal choices. Fortunate are we who had mothers who wanted to bring new life into the world! We are the fruit of their choice.

Mothers are special because of their nurturing instinct, which is innate to a certain degree. Watch even a small girl as she cuddles her doll. Every small girl oohs and aahs at babies! In a home where a girl's femininity is valued and even encouraged, that sense of nurture matures until as a young woman she holds her own child. Children deprived of a mother's nurture—the cuddling, the gentle speech, the soft tones—sense that lack throughout their lives. Fortunate are we who had mothers who nurtured us through life.

Mothers are special because of their service. Early in the morning, throughout the day, and late into the night, mothers are tending to their children. "I need to feed the kids, make sure they are properly dressed, get them a snack before the game . . ." The needs of the children are endless, but so is the mother's desire to provide the necessary care. Fortunate are we who had mothers who provided that kind of gentle care for us.

Mothers are special because they never stop loving us. They love us through childhood into adult life. They love us when we make good choices. Even though they may be frustrated at our bad choices, they love us nonetheless. Harold Morris spent years in prison for crime. Many people gave up on him, but not his mother. After his release Morris wrote, "A mother was the only person near and dear to most inmates. Mothers offered a special kind of love because they loved you no matter what . . . Other family members would disown you because you'd disgraced them . . . But a mother would cry herself to sleep, blaming herself for her son's crimes. She would never stop loving. I was convinced that nobody was fully an animal while he still had a mother living" (Beyond the Barriers [Nashville: W Publishing Group, 1987], p. 37). Fortunate are we who had mothers who loved us no matter what!

Mothers are special because of the sacrifices they make on our behalf. Birthing us, nurturing us, serving us, and loving us are all sacrifices moms make for their children. But most moms don't think of it as sacrificing. They love their kids and want to do what is right and best for them. They don't begrudge giving up their time, their energy, their desires, and sometimes even their health for their little ones. The heart of a loving mother is much like the heart of Jesus—seeking to serve and not be served. We are all blessed who had mothers who served us.

Mothers are special because they joyfully acknowledge anything their children do to show even the slightest appreciation for them. How many mothers have put a vase of weeds on the table for display because that is what their little ones brought them as a gift? How many refrigerators display the art of a three-year-old? How much soggy cereal, cold eggs, and burnt toast have mothers eaten with a smile on Saturday mornings because their kids wanted to play chef?

This is part of my list of why moms are special, drawn from experiences with my own mother, my wife's mom, and my children's mother. I hope you have your list. Life can never be as sweet as it is meant by God to be unless we can look back with gratitude at the great work done in our lives by mothers who bore us, served us, and, as we went off on our own, prayed for us.

GRANDPARENTS

As iron sharpens iron, so one man sharpens another.
—Proverbs 27:17

"Where are you from?" I asked the older couple I had just met in Yellowstone National Park.

"We are from Toledo, Ohio. We come out here to Yellowstone every couple of years."

"You must like it a lot," I responded.

"Yes, it is beautiful here. But that is not the main reason we come out. As our grandchildren get old enough to be away from home for a couple of weeks, we take them on a long trip out west. It gives us special "grandparent" time with them. We try to stay close to all of our grandchildren, and a trip like this really cements our relationship with them."

"Wow" was about all I could muster at first. "That is a wonderful idea, and a great experience for you and your grandchildren. I'll bet your grandchildren will never forget what you are doing for them! This experience and your continued involvement in their lives will help mold their character and impact their future in so many positive ways."

This was a real conversation, similar to numerous others I've had. A travel camper occupied with gray-haired adults and two or three smiling children signaled that this was a grandparent-grandchild trip in Yellowstone.

Grandparents can create experiences like this for their grandchildren to have fun together. But more is happening than just fun. Grandma and Grandpa are in a dynamic, lively relationship with their grandchildren. They will never be bored, even in retirement.

Something even more important is happening on these trips: the grandparents are passing on a legacy of what they value and hold dear, such as travel, working, saving money, and being with family. Teaching and passing on the legacy is not reduced to lectures or reprimands but grows out of the shared experiences between grandparents and grandchildren.

I suspect there has always been a "gap" between the older generations and the younger, especially since the late 1800s when technology changed the way almost everything is done, from farming to cooking to sewing clothes. With these technological changes have come changes in the way we view work, time management, family, and values.

But no matter what changes have been experienced in the way society moves today, one thing remains unchanged: we all need connection with people. We all need to feel loved, respected, appreciated, and needed. No one is exempt. So, grandparents, your role in closing the "generation gap" cannot be overestimated. Bonding with your grandchildren when they are young and reinforcing that bond as they grow and mature is building a life, forging a destiny, and shaping an eternity. In fact, with grandparents and grandchildren who are in meaningful relationship, there is no generation gap. The older loves the younger, the younger respects and listens to the older. Both generations give and receive. The generation in the middle, the moms and dads of the youngsters, are sure glad the grandmas and grandpas are there!

I'll never forget the conversations I had with my grandfather when I was a young teen. Grandpa had retired and was living in a trailer on our small farm. On Saturday mornings I'd go to Grandma's and Grandpa's to visit, to eat the pie and pastries they made, and to listen. Grandpa would tell stories about his life during the Depression. He told me what my dad was like as a boy. He shared with me why he made the decision to become a Christian when he was over fifty years old. He explained to me the things he was learning in his daily Bible study. I remember thinking, "If being a Christian was that important to Grandpa, it must be something I should think more about, too." I am confident that his influence in those years were instrumental in my decision to become a preacher. My life today is still affected by this man, even though he went on to meet the Lord over twenty years ago.

Grandparents, be involved in the lives of your grandchildren. That doesn't mean you have to take them on a trip to Yellowstone National Park. Not everyone's budget will allow for trips like that. But can you afford a trip to a local baseball game, complete with hot dogs and a cheese pretzel? If your grandchildren live a long distance away, pick some kids from your church or your neighborhood and become a "stepgrandparent." The positive, long-term impact may be as important for you as for the children. "As iron sharpens iron, so through loving interaction do grandparents sharpen their grandchildren."

SEE YOU AT THE BALLPARK

Be sure you know the condition of your flocks, give careful attention to your herds; for riches do not endure forever, and a crown is not secure for all generations.

—Proverbs 27:23–24

Many of the proverbs were written for family farmers and ranchers. This proverb addresses a small rancher whose livelihood is staked to the health of his cattle or sheep. It is only through tireless devotion to his herd that the rancher can ensure the health of his animals and the financial survival of his family. Drought, disease, and wild animals are always on the prowl looking for unprotected beasts to assail! The rancher must keep watch to ward off the attackers.

The principle of daily diligence applies to all of life. Faithful performance in our jobs is necessary whether it be feeding animals or entering data into a computer. Daily diligence by Mom and Dad means being alert to dangers facing our families. Parents who are too busy, children without supervision, and television that is not monitored are modern assaults on the health of a family. Parental diligence demands that we give careful attention to "our herds," our families. Look for the signs of health and happiness. Do the children walk through the house and sing? Do they devise simple games to occupy themselves? Do they listen to and obey the voice of Mom and Dad? Is "I love you" frequently heard? Does bedtime mean hugs, stories, and being tucked in? These are signs of happy and contented children. When their behavior becomes disruptive, can it be quickly stilled by Mom and Dad's strong presence and voice?

To be able to have this kind of influence in a home, Mom and Dad must be in the home. They must be active in the family. Children left to raise themselves will . . . but not very effectively. Their lack of discipline and maturity will set the tone for the family, creating disorder and chaos. Only the loving presence of Mom and Dad can instill order and peace.

With the demands on their schedules and their resources, parents are hard pressed to find the time and energy required to give adequate attention to family health. Jobs, financial demands, insecurity, and exhaustion plague all of us, robbing us of energy and confidence. Every parent struggles with these assaults, but the successful parents persevere, consistently applying care and attention to their flocks.

As our children grow older, spending time with them isn't as simple as reading a bedtime story or kicking a soccer ball in the yard. In high school it means traveling across the state to watch them swing a bat or fly over a hurdle. Considerable time and money are involved! Is it worth it? Does this have anything to do with giving attention to our "herd"? Listen to these words from a young friend of mine: "My dad has never been to one of my games."

A high school senior shared these words with Cheryl and me as he was showing us the trophies of his baseball career. His pitching struck fear into opponents and confidence into his team. He claimed many victories and received numerous awards. As he looked at the trophy in his hands, a note of sadness came over his face, and he softly said, "My dad has never been to one of my games."

Missing four years of his son's games was merely symptomatic of this dad's failure to monitor the health of his family. He simply wasn't present. His son could not bask in the glory of his baseball success because he was silently grieving that he couldn't share it with his dad. Dad's inattentiveness bred hurt and bitterness in the heart of his family. His herd suffered.

Think about Proverbs 27:23–24 applied to the family: "Be sure you know the condition of your family, give careful attention to your children; for closeness does not endure, and family health is not secure for all generations." Healthy families are not only possible; they are promised by God, if we approach our role as parents with daily diligence, feeding, teaching, and nurturing our young ones. If that includes attending their sports activities, then I'll see you at the ballpark.

ROD OF CORRECTION

The rod of correction imparts wisdom, but a child left to himself disgraces his mother.
—Proverbs 29:15

Discipline your son, and he will give you peace; he will bring delight to your soul.
—Proverbs 29:17

There are some passages in the Bible that are hard to apply today. They were written for a particular time and may not be applied literally today. Deuteronomy 21:18–21 is one of those texts. "If a man has a stubborn and rebellious son who does not obey his father and mother and will not listen to them when they discipline him, his father and mother shall take hold of him and bring him to the elders at the gate of his town. They shall say to the elders, 'This son of ours is stubborn and rebellious. He will not obey us. He is a profligate and a drunkard.' Then all the men of his town shall stone him to death. You must purge the evil from among you. All Israel will hear of it and be afraid."

This text is hard to apply today. How many of us advocate the stoning to death of a child who was repeatedly disobedient? I don't know anyone who would. But there are some applications of this passage we should give attention.

This passage, as well as the Proverbs texts, underline how serious God is about children obeying and respecting their parents. The stubborn and rebellious son in this passage is not a teenager who occasionally loses his cool around the house or slips up once and awhile. It is a young man who willfully violates his parents' code and who demonstrates flagrant disobedience.

This young man was regarded in ancient Israel as incorrigible. He was not to be treated lightly. He was not to be coddled. Counseling was not an option. He was to be disposed of, but not as an act of anger or vengeance on the part of the hurting parents. He was to be punished as an act of judicial function by the city fathers or elders.

This is a severe punishment, very severe. But this highlights how seriously God regards respect for one's parents. Disrespect for parents can lead to the disintegration of respect in all aspects of society. A society devoid of respect for one another and for authority cannot function very long, at least not in a healthy way.

God's concern for proper attitudes and behavior on the part of children toward their parents is for the healthy functioning of the family as well as the healthy ordering of all society. If families are allowed to fall apart, entire societies can disintegrate right along with them. Maintaining respect and order at home promotes respect and order in the world.

These passages speak not only of the proper attitudes and behavior of children; they also speaks volumes about what parents should and should not allow to go on in their homes. Small children are often allowed to sass their parents because the little guys are so cute. But it is not cute when they are sixteen years old. If you don't want a sixteen-year-old to shout you down, call you names, or belittle you, don't tolerate it from them when they are little! Age twelve months to three years are the critical times we parents have to instill within our children proper respect for us.

Also, when we tell our small children to do something, we should demand compliance with what we say. Telling a small child to pick up his shoes and then having to pick them up for him because he refuses to is training the child to do what he wants. We shouldn't be surprised then when at age sixteen, this child refuses to drive safely or be home by ten just because we tell him to. If we did not train this child to obey at age two, and we did not really expect him to, what makes us think he will obey us when he is sixteen? We have trained him to do what he wants, not what we say. Such permissiveness robs a child of security and self-esteem and robs a family of peace and delight.

"Discipline your son, and he will give you peace; he will bring delight to your soul." A disciplined child will also bring delight to the entire community.

A DISCERNING SON

"He who keeps the law is a discerning son, but a companion of gluttons disgraces his father."

—Proverbs 28:7

All of us who are parents want the lives of our children to reflect the morals and values we try to instill within them. We would like to see them be respectful, be law abiding, be conservative with their spending habits, and be kind to others. This is how most of us try to live, and to see these values at work in the lives of our children is gratifying.

The child who honors the teaching and will of the parents and lives such a disciplined life is called "a discerning son." To be discerning means the child thinks through things. When invited by friends to go to a party, he stops and thinks, "Will this party reflect the values of my parents? Will there be alcohol there? Will I really be able to resist the temptation to drink? What if the police come and I get arrested? Even if the police don't come, do I want my reputation sullied by being in an environment that can not feed my Spirit, but in fact may do it great damage? Will my being at that party reflect well on my parents, my church and my God?"

This ability to discern between competing issues of pleasure or discipline is not limited to just parties, but to every aspect of life. "What classes do I need to take in high school to prepare me for college? What classes in college do I need to take to prepare me for a career? What career choice would allow me to grow and develop without having to compromise any of my convictions? What kind of friends will encourage my personal ethics and convictions? What is a godly way to save and spend the money I make?"

Granted, this is a lot of mental work. It takes a lot of thinking, a lot of personal introspection and a lot of time. There are people willing to make these kinds of investments, but there are people who are not so willing.

Thank goodness for those children who are discerning and keep the law. The "law" that Proverbs speaks of here could be the law of the land. That would mean that the discerning son or daughter obeys the local legal codes. But the "law" here probably refers to the teaching of the parents. The reason Proverbs calls this boy a discerning son is because he has listened to mom and dad and adheres to their advice and teaching about morals, proper behavior and career choices.

Parents are proud of a discerning son or daughter. It gives both mom and dad confidence and satisfaction that their lessons over two decades have taken root and have produced a disciplined and fruitful lifestyle in their offspring. The other option this verse discusses that kids can take is not so pleasant and satisfying. The other path a child can take is to be a "companion of gluttons."

It seems rather odd that this proverb contrasts a discerning son and a friend of gluttons. What is a friend of gluttons? This is probably a reference to a son that rejects the teaching of the parents and becomes gluttonous and profligate. He squanders the family resources and becomes a pleasure seeker who spends money carelessly. He may party, drive under the influence of alcohol and wreck the family car. The police are called in, lawyers are consulted and insurance premiums go up. If the son doesn't turn from this kind of rebellious behavior soon, it could become habitual and disgrace the family's name in the community. That is why Proverbs says, "a companion of gluttons disgraces his father."

Nothing gives parents greater joy than to see their children make wise, wholesome choices. Every parent can "amen" this plea from another verse in Proverbs: "May your father and mother be glad; may she who gave you birth rejoice!" (Proverbs 23:25).

We can't guarantee the paths our children will take, but if we are actively involved in their lives, teaching and modeling wise behavior, we always have a prayer that the lessons will take root in their hearts.

PAMPERING CHILDREN

> If a man pampers his servant from youth, he will bring grief in the end.
>
> —Proverbs 29:21

Substitute the word "children" for "servant" in this verse, and we will see wisdom here for parenting. Children need some pampering, especially when they are babies. To be held, fed, and cuddled is an experience that binds the baby to the mother and the mother to the baby. As soon as he summons the courage, the dad can enter into this pampering experience and enjoy the bonding process as well. Virtually every need of a healthy baby is met by this loving, protective parenting of Mom and Dad.

How long does this intense pampering process last? Some parents maintain intense pampering of their children all their lives. When their baby is floundering around on weak legs and falls, Mom and Dad run to pick him up and coddle him, trying to protect him from the frustration and pain of falling. When the child is playing and gets bumped and cries, Mom and Dad pick the child up and cry, "Poor baby, you have a bump." When the child gets picked last for team sports on the playground, Mom and Dad call the school and complain. When the teenager is not invited to outings with his peer group, Mom and Dad call the other parents and reprimand them for raising inconsiderate children. When this young adult gets married and runs into some relational problems, Mom and Dad blame the son—or daughter-in-law for not being the kind of spouse their lovely baby needs. "If a man pampers his servant (or child) from youth, he will bring grief in the end."

I've seen children raised with this kind of excessive pampering. It is called "being spoiled." Some parents see it as their duty to protect their child from any kind of pain or disappointment. We do need to teach our children and protect them from the serious dangers of cars, fireplaces, kitchen utensils, vicious dogs, and other things that can seriously harm them. But we also have to let them experience the frustration of falling, or they won't know the success of getting back up again. We have to let them experience the bruises when they play with other children, or they will never learn that bumps are a natural part of any relationship. We have to help them assess why they are the last to be chosen at team sports; they maybe unskilled and need more practice or they may be poor sports and need to grow up. We have to help them understand why they may not be invited to peer outings. If they are spoiled the other kids may not want them around. If Mom and Dad have so protected their children that they expect everyone else to shower them with that same pampering care, the kids will be sorely disappointed, because it won't happen. If they don't learn that by the time they are teenagers, they surely will when their husband or wife refuses to treat them like spoiled children.

Growing up is tough. It is hard for us parents as we watch our children hurt and we have to decide whether to move in to help or to let the children bear the pain on their own, work it out, and grow through it. It is hard on the child. Bumps and bruises are not fun; but if children aren't allowed to experience them when they are little, they will be ill prepared for them when they are grown. The time will come when Mom and Dad won't be there to protect them.

It is sad to watch a small child cry in frustration because things are not going his way. But it is harder to watch an adult cry because he wasn't allowed to learn that lesson as a child, and he still thinks everything is supposed to run smoothly in life. "If a man pampers his servant (or child) from youth, he will bring grief in the end." Do your kids a favor: let them experience the knocks of life when they are young so they will be prepared for them when they are older.

THE AMAZING METS

She watches over the affairs of her household and does not eat the
bread of idleness. Her children arise and call her blessed.

—Proverbs 31:27–28

I was born a Mets fan. As a kid I knew the names, statistics, and
memorable plays of the Mets' players, such as Ron Swaboda's rolling-tumble
catch. I began watching baseball on TV with my grandfather, and I was with
him when we saw Ron made that phenomenal catch. "Did you see that!
Did you see that!" Grandpa shouted.

Since we didn't have a television set at the time, we were glued to the radio
in 1969 when the Mets won the World Series. My mother helped me make
a poster that read: World Champ Mets. I stood on the side of Rural Route
5 in Sutton, Vermont, proudly holding up the sign to vehicles passing by.

But the real story about my fascination with the Mets took almost a
whole summer to unfold, and it involved my mother. I read a book to her.
Out loud. As Mom went about her work in the kitchen, I sat in a chair and
read to her the exciting story of how the Mets won the World Series. The
book was appropriately entitled The Amazing Mets.

Some things have changed since that summer of 1970. I'm not a Mets
fan anymore, and other than an occasional story, I don't read many sports
books.

But some things have remained unchanged since that summer. I still
like to read. I still enjoy lazy moments in the summer. And I do still enjoy
watching a good baseball game.

Other things have intensified: I will always honor the memory of my
mother for the time and energy she always had for Jim, Bob, Carol, and me.
She surely spent that summer "watching over the affairs of her household"
even if that included listening all summer to stories about baseball. I'm
sure my selection of The Amazing Mets was not her first choice for reading
material! But it was my choice, so she listened.

I wound up learning more that summer than what Tom Seaver's pitching
record was or if Bud Harrelson was the best shortstop ever. I learned patience.
Mom had to have a good dose of that! I learned that love means you don't
insist on what you want, but you consider what someone else wants or
needs. I learned that listening is a precious art, a great gift of love. I learned

that kids take a lot of time, and they need that time. I learned that reading is a better way to pass the hours than watching TV. I learned that parents who care give their time and energy for the benefit of their kids. I learned that the summer of 1970 spent in the kitchen reading The Amazing Mets to my mother wasn't really about baseball at all.

ACCEPTING GOD'S WILL

NO FEAR

Whoever listens to me will live in safety and be at ease, without fear of harm.

—Proverbs 1:33

This proverb is a bold statement of confidence and security. It speaks of the strength we draw from living in relationship with God and in his wisdom. Those outside of God and his wisdom live in foolishness, disharmony, dysfunction, and fear. My heart goes out to them. "Wisdom calls aloud in the street" (Prov. 1:20) to them, but they refuse to listen. But for those who listen and respond to God and his claim on our lives, there is safety and ease. We can be confident and secure.

Proverbs 29:25 is another positive verse about the confidence a relationship with God grants us. "Fear of man will prove to be a snare, but whoever trusts in the Lord is kept safe."

The first half of this proverb acknowledges that some people live with fear. "Fear of man" can have two reference points. One point of reference is the person who does the fearing. He may lack confidence and fear the limitations of his own abilities or character. He may realize he lacks self-control or self-discipline and fears he will commit sin or do something foolish. He is experiencing self-paralysis from his own insecurity.

The other referent of the fear is someone or something outside of the man who is afraid. He may fear circumstances beyond his control, or he may fear strong and intimidating personalities (Roland Murphy, WBC:

Proverbs [Nashville: Thomas Nelson, 1998], 22:233). He may doubt his own internal strength to stand up to a manipulator and say no to his intimidations. Either way, this man's fear will be a snare to his life. It will drag him down, stifle him, and starve his joy. If he could place himself in God's hands, this man of fear would find confidence in the safety God provides.

These proverbs vibrate with possibility for people today. Karol K. Truman, in Feelings Buried Alive Never Die (St. George, UT: Olympus Distributing, 1991), claims that over forty million people in the United States suffer with some form of phobia. A phobia is "an obsessive, irrational fear or anxiety." A person living in fear is actually living either in the past or in the future, not in the present. A person experiencing fear is tormented by something that happened in the past and lives in dread that it could happen again in the future. But much of this person's fear is an illusion. "The illusion is worry—what if—and our unconscious imagining takes it from there and runs wild" (p. 167).

Worry stems from the past and is projected into the future. The person living in fear is always looking back over his shoulder or is looking ahead. Neither glance is joyful or hopeful. Both are characterized by fear, loathing, and paralysis. Because this person is living in the past or in the future, he cannot experience joy today. For one living in fear, the present is nothing but the incubator for the trauma of tomorrow. So the fearful person is always edgy, judgmental, temperamental, and angry. His stress levels rise intolerably high, feeding the edginess and anger. All the joy is sucked out of life. Happiness is denied. Gratitude is starved. How can a person be joyful, happy, or thankful if he expects a tragedy at any moment?

What is the solution? Trusting in God. Putting our faith in him. Placing our lives in his care. There are no guarantees that everything will go the way we like or want. But we can have the confidence that God's protective care will see us safely through whatever trying circumstances come our way. We can bask in the safety and ease God's grace is ready to grant us. We can wake up each morning with positive expectations that with God on our side, there is nothing to fear. Trust conquers fear, and faith trumps anxiety. We can live in the present and experience all the joy God meant for us to have. "Whoever listens to God will live in safety and be at ease, without fear of harm."

TRUSTING OUR CAGE

Trust in the Lord with all your heart and lean not on your own understanding.

—Proverbs 3:5

Two key words appear in this verse: trust and understand. To explain them, let me tell you about my two miniature hamsters.

My pet hamsters have the good life. They are in a cage with plenty of food, water, and clean shavings my daughters put in there. They are in a climate-controlled room. Could you ask for any better? But these critters don't understand how good they have it. They are always wanting to get out. Why? Outside lurks all kinds of unspeakable dangers to these furry little rodents. A cat. A dog. The rocking chair. My big feet. Why would they risk their lives with these dangers? Because they simply don't understand.

Here is the irony: the only real danger these miniature hamsters face is their attempts to get out of the cage. The cage is made of thin little bars. They climb them and hang from the ceiling of the cage. One hamster did that and lost his grip with his front claws. He hung suspended and dislocated his leg at the hip. A call to the vet (at the behest of my daughter Kristin) was met with the suggestion that I try to reset the leg myself. I tried, but my numerous attempts met with failure. The other suggestion from the vet: leave the animal alone for a few days and see if he could reset it himself. He did. That hamster is fine now, and is back climbing the walls of his cage.

The hamsters continue their attempts to get out because they don't understand the danger on the outside. Nor do they understand how important it is to trust us that their greatest safety and happiness lies within the walls of that cage. Sure, it is confining, but it is safe. The creature comforts of food and water are always close at hand. What would they do on the outside? How would they make their way in the world that lies beyond their cage? What awaits them is hunger and thirst or an unpleasant encounter with a kitty.

It is striking how much we humans resemble these rodents. God gives us a choice—we can live within the confines of a "cage" that he has for us, or we can climb out and roam free. But to stay within the cage means we have to understand God's desire for us and we have to trust that his way is really best.

I really don't like to think of God's will for us as being a cage or as being confining, but his will certainly does restrict us. One of God's restrictions is behavior limits he places on us. God does not want us hurting others, committing murder, gossiping, or besmirching another person's name. God does not want us engaging in adultery or in any moral sin against our spouse or even our future spouse. These are behavioral limitations, much like the walls of a cage. But there is more . . . God also has attitudinal restrictions for us. He wants to stop sin even before the bad behavior breaks out. God does not want to us to show attitudes of hate, envy, jealousy, lust, bitterness, or rage. In time a bad attitude will give way to bad behavior, and someone will get hurt.

Here is our cage. Can we accept it? To live within these confines is limiting, yes, but at the same time it is safer for us spiritually, emotionally, and physically. A young person who begins marriage sexually pure has an advantage over someone who played the field. To step outside of these confines invites sorrow and grief, pain and guilt. Ultimately, living outside the confines of God's restrictions invites death.

The next verse in Proverbs says, "In all your ways acknowledge him, and he will make your paths straight." That doesn't mean that everything will go perfectly for us, but it does imply that God's blessing will be upon our lives. "Trust in the Lord with all your heart and lean not on your own understanding."

LYING LIPS

The Lord detests lying lips, but he delights in men who are truthful.
—Proverbs 12:22

We categorize sin. To us, some sins are worse than others. We do not justify kidnaping, child abuse, or murder. We do not accept any rationale for such behavior. But there are categories of sin that we tolerate, such as lying, gossiping, hatred, jealousy, and selfishness. God, on the other hand, condemns these "lesser" sins just as he does kidnaping, child abuse, or murder. In fact, they are mentioned even more times in the Bible than the other three "big" sins. So why do we have a higher tolerance level for these sins? My guess is that these sins are so prevalent and we are guilty of them. I have never kidnaped anyone, abused a child, or committed murder. But I have lied and committed the other sins. Maybe you can see why we are more tolerant of them. These are our sins. Since we are good people, surely these sins can't be that bad. But then we find this sobering verse: "The Lord detests lying lips." Just how much does he hate them?

Years ago a Christian husband and wife felt a tug to do more in their service to God. They had recently acquired a bit of cash and decided to donate a large portion of it to God. Their desire was for the money to be used in feeding the hungry or preaching the Gospel. Very noble intentions. This couple took the money to one of the local Christian ministers.

There is always need in the kingdom for more money to feed the hungry, aid the down-and-out, and send missionaries into the world. All it takes to acquire the needed funds is for Christians to have deeper pockets and generous hearts. But it is hard, isn't it? Most of us have an abundance of bills and accumulated debts. We have a list of things we need plus a list of things we want. By the time money gets apportioned to all of these areas, how much do we have left for the important work of God's kingdom? Not enough.

So it must have been a glorious day when this man took a large chunk of his accumulated cash and laid it at the feet of the preacher. I imagine the preacher was ecstatic! When a family gives 10 percent to the Lord, we regard that as serious stewardship! But when someone gives 60 or 70 percent, that breaks records!

But this preacher was not impressed with the gift. He wasn't moved to lavish praise on this man and woman. He didn't hold them up as a positive example of financial stewardship. Instead, he heaped fierce words of judgment on the couple. "Ananias, how is it that Satan has so filled your heart that you have lied to the Holy Spirit and have kept for yourself some of the money you received for the land? Didn't it belong to you before it was sold? And after it was sold, wasn't the money at your disposal? What made you think of doing such a thing? You have not lied to men but to God." At that, Ananias fell down and died. Three hours later, his wife, Sapphira, suffered the same fate (Acts 5:3–9).

What was the sin of Ananias and Sapphira? Greed? No. They didn't give enough? That wasn't it. Their sin was lying. They gave part of the money they received for the land, but they gave the impression they gave all of it. Even though it was a large portion, perhaps over 50 percent, the preacher, Simon Peter, didn't get excited about it. He got angry that the two contributors lied. "The Lord detests lying lips, but he delights in men who are truthful."

We may lay a heavier stress on the abhorrence of some sins over others. But we best be careful. We need to register sin by God's standard, not ours.

To God, lying is a great abhorrence because it works against the truth and against community. People cannot live together in meaningful relationship when they lie to one another. Families cannot function in an atmosphere of lying. Churches and Christians cannot be a positive light for God if they lie or tolerate liars. "The Lord detests lying lips, but he delights in men who are truthful." This is a hard truth, but it is the truth: guard your lips and keep your words sound.

WISHING, ANXIETY, AND HOPE

> Hope deferred makes the heart sick, but a longing fulfilled is a tree of life.
>
> —Proverbs 13:12

How do we face the future? Some people wish for their future to be a certain way. They daydream or fantasize about how rich they will be, how popular, how successful. They may spend very little time in actual preparation for their future. Studying, working, or saving money seems useless to them. People who engage in too much wishful thinking tend to be undisciplined and lazy. They may be very talented and capable, but they lack the character to summon all of these positive traits into a constructive, meaningful direction.

Others face the future with anxiety. Anxiety is fear of the unknown, the uncertain, the unproven. Who has been to the future? Who knows what it is like? Who can tell me what is there for me? Insecurity is a major cause for feeling anxious. One is insecure about what the future holds and one's ability to meet it.

Think of the "threats" teenagers hear about in the news and that awaits them in the future: war, spiraling debt, rampant crime, topsy-turvy economy, taxes, inflation, and a high divorce rate. Mmmm. I'm feeling a bit anxious myself just writing this paragraph!

Is it just a coincidence that one of the favorite literary forms of youth is science fiction, a genre based in future fantasy that feeds the wishful thinking of youth? Or is it a coincidence that drug use and emotional breakdown (and even suicide) are so common for them as a means of "dealing" with the anxiety-causing events thrusted upon them?

Wishing and anxiety are not the only responses we have regarding the future, though these are the only responses some people know about. Fortunately for the Christian, there is another response: hope.

Hope is not fantasizing or wishful thinking. Nor is hope the denial that the future does indeed harbor a degree of uncertainty, maybe even including pain and loss. Hope does not simply say, "The future will be okay because God is in control and therefore I don't have to do anything." That is presuming upon God!

What is hope? "Hope is a response to the future which has its foundation in the promises of God. It looks at the future as time for the completion of God's promise" (Thanks to Eugene Peterson for this quote and his ideas on Christian hope found in his book, Like Dew Your Youth [Grand Rapids: Eerdemans, 1976], p. 72). Hope is faith in God translated into calm perspective and faithful service.

Hope does believe that God is in our future, but it does not presume upon God nor obligate him to act in accordance with our desires. Hope in God's presence energizes us to face our future with confidence (Heb. 13:5–6), with commitment to biblical ethics (2 Pet. 1:5–9), with an agenda of godly works (Eph. 2:10), with Spirit-filled character (Gal. 5:22–24) and with the assurance of God's presence (Ps. 121).

Hope is what sustained Jesus in the garden. Was Jesus wishful that the cross would just go away or that it wouldn't hurt? Didn't he experience some anxiety, which is why he prayed and sweated profusely? But he knew God was with him and would see him through to victory, no matter what the pain on that journey.

Hope can and will do the same for us. We need to share that with our children. But before we can, we parents need to have that hope. Hope . . . God's gift to his believers. Hope "fulfilled is a tree of life."

JESUS SAVES

Even in death the righteous have a refuge.
—Proverbs 14:32b

Death doesn't have the final word. "For God did not send his Son into the world to condemn the world, but to save the world through him" (John 3:17). All Christians believe that Jesus saves us. But how? There are three basic explanations of how God works in Jesus to save us.

One, Jesus is the victor. In this explanation Jesus is seen as doing battle with sin and the devil throughout his life. Think of Jesus' encounter with the devil in the episode entitled, "The Temptation of Jesus." Three times the devil challenged Jesus to turn from his spiritual work. But Jesus knew he was at battle, and he resisted and fought the devil. Three times Jesus turned to scripture for his ammunition and told the devil, "It is written" (Matt. 4:1–11).

Jesus' battle against the devil culminated in his victory at the cross. Death, the realm of Satan, couldn't hold Jesus, so he arose victoriously. Now we, the followers of Jesus, share in this victory. First Corinthians 15:57 says, "But thanks be to God. He gives us the victory through our Lord Jesus Christ."

Two, Jesus is our substitute. This view sees the tremendous weight of sin that burdens human beings, smothering them under a terrible weight of condemnation. "The wages of sin is death." What a burden we bear! But we have a savior, Jesus, who serves as a substitute for us. Paul says, "Christ redeemed us from the curse of the law by becoming a curse for us" (Gal. 3:13). The clearest statement about this is found in 2 Corinthians 5:21, "God made him who had no sin to be sin for us . . ."

Instead of us having to bear the burden and condemnation of our sin, Jesus did for us. He is our substitute.

Third, Jesus is our example. Jesus is the victor over the power of sin and the devil. Jesus is our substitute for sin and death. These are both objective realities to show what God has done for us. But Christ is more than victor and substitute. He is also our example.

Once we have been freed from the damnation of sin, what next? Those of us who are Christians must be honest with ourselves and with those who are not Christians. We still have problems in our lives, don't we? Even though we have been saved from sin, we still struggle with sins. Here is where the example of Christ has power for our lives.

Christ Jesus is our example of love and sacrifice. He gave everything—his time, his love, his service, his life. Nothing was held back in service to the father for our good. Paul uses this example of Jesus to say, "Live a life of love, just as Christ loved us and gave himself up for us" (Eph. 5:2). The sacrificial love of Jesus empowers us to live sacrificially for others.

Jesus is our victor, substitute, and example. Jesus covers the bases for us. He conquered sin and the devil. He gave himself on the cross to satisfy God's demand for justice, and he gives us an example in how to live.

"We are saved, therefore, not simply because Jesus pays the price for us, or becomes the perfect substitution for us, but also because he teaches us how to love. And, in teaching us how to love, Jesus teaches us how to live" (Stacy Patty, Theology Matters, ed. by Gary Holloway et al., [Joplin, MO: College Press, 1998], p. 51). Because of Jesus, "even in death the righteous have a refuge."

WORK

The laborer's appetite works for him; his hunger drives him on.
Proverbs 16:26

Hunger is a good thing. Hunger is God's way of informing the body that it is ready for some more nutrition. Hunger is also God's way of nudging the body out of bed and out to work. The Sage says that hunger actually works for us, motivating us to earn our living.

The best form of motivation is internal. You can motivate me by encouraging me, giving me reasons to work harder, or, if you are my boss, by threatening to fire me. But, as any coach knows, the best form of motivation is that which wells up inside a person, as when an athlete is motivated from within to try harder, press forward, and give 110%. This person will persevere even when the coach's enthusiasm may begin to wane!

This principle from sports is true for any worthy endeavor, even for working a job. There are days when we would like to roll over, block the sunlight with our covers, and sleep another hour. But there are bills to pay and food to buy. These basic needs drive us to get up and go to work. That is a good thing! The laborer's appetite works for him.

Besides having this very practical motivation to buy food, work also has an important theological motivation. The apostle Paul wrote, "If a man will not work, he shall not eat." (2 Thessalonians 3:10) When God expressed his care for the OT Israelites by moving them into the promised land, he didn't promise to give them full refrigerators and cupboards. He promised them land and water and fruit trees, but they had to work the land, water the crops and prune and harvest the trees. What God promised the Israelites was the opportunity for honest work.

Work is good. Sometimes it can even be fun. My son Wes worked for my brother's law firm in Bozeman, MT for a year. One day a partner in the firm gave Wes a camera and said, "Go take some pictures of that lake near Yellowstone National Park. We'll need them for our case." Wes spent most of the day driving to the Yellowstone area and taking pictures of the country. He got paid for that. Another day he had to drive through the mountains and deliver a document to a court. That took a couple of hours. When he returned, the partner had another document for him to take to the same court. He asked Wes, "Do you mind going back?" Wes thought, "Do I mind? You are going to pay me to drive through these beautiful mountains, and you ask if that bothers me?"

Not all work is that inviting and desirable. I worked all four years I was in college. As a freshman I was on work study and had to clean the Milan Sitka building. That included cleaning all the bathrooms. When I had to leave campus one day to visit family, I tried to find a student to take my place and get my pay that day. I asked several students, "Would you like to work for me Friday?" They all said, "Sure! Where do you work? The library? The cafeteria?" "No," I said. "I clean Milan Sitka." "The bathrooms, too?" they would ask. They all declined. One guy even added, "I don't need the money that badly. My allowance comes next week anyway." My friend said this as he was lying on his bunk in the middle of the day.

I think this young man's parents did him a disservice. Sure, you can work so much at college that you don't get to enjoy the college experience, and there is much there to enjoy. But the college experience is about education, and part of that education is learning that work is noble, honorable, and worthy. It services the practical function of providing our food and the theological function of honoring God. Don't neglect this important principle in the upbringing of your children or in the exercise of your own responsibilities: "The laborer's appetite works for him; his hunger drives him on."

INSPIRATION

Listen to advice and accept instruction, and in the end you will be wise.

—Proverbs 19:20

Stories of successful men and women inspire us. The stories of statesmen, athletes, and religious leaders can motivate us to stretch ourselves to live at higher levels.

The story of Eva Krutein is about a twenty-year-old woman with an indomitable spirit. Her autobiography Eva's War: A True Story of Survival is about her struggle for survival in war-torn Europe. Eva left Danzig, Germany, in the 1940s to flee the advance of the Russian army. She boarded a ship with nothing but her baby, her purse, one suitcase, and a baby carriage. She changed ships just in time—the ship she left one day was torpedoed the next day by Russian submarines. Ten thousand civilians lost their lives in the Baltic Sea. But Eva hung on. For the next couple of years Eva struggled for herself and her daughter, living in refugee centers and bombed-out cities. She was frequently hungry. In her first two years of marriage, she was with her husband for only two months. Her story is inspiring. If a young woman with a baby can survive such insurmountable odds as an advancing army, with no food and plenty of loneliness and heartache, what do I have to complain about!

There are great stories of inspiration in the Bible. There is a story about a boy who is adopted and raised in a foreign environment. Later he makes a connection to his own ethnic people and at age forty, breaks away from his adopted culture. For forty years, he wanders in the wilderness tending sheep. At age eighty he is called by God to active ministry. He is still a shepherd, but now his flock is people. He leads his flock through decades of a dry, parched existence in the desert, all the time trying to direct their eyes towards the new life ahead of them. This man, Moses, inspires in us greater trust in God's promises and faithfulness in adversity.

You can read of another young man hiding in the desert with a group of ragtag ne'er-do-wells. They had their own robbers' roost, something akin to the wilderness hideouts Jesse James and other adventurers had in the Wild West. They made their living robbing from other people. The leader of their group had better morals and character than this, but he fell upon very hard times. He was driven into the desert by the king's envy, so it wasn't safe for anyone to help him. But he never completely forgot God. Even when times were terribly dismal, he remembered his early godly training. He wrote poems during this period which were later collected and even today are read or sung in the worship service of churches. This young man kept his faith, and one day the Lord honored it by raising him up to be king. You should recognize this man as David.

Stories like this are in the Bible to serve as models for us. They tell what we can do and what we can become or how we can overcome. No one would have guessed that young Moses would lead the Israelites out of Egypt to the Promised Land or that David would lead them after they got there. No one knew but God. He knew what these men could overcome and what they could become. And he knows the same thing about you.

Have you read any good biographies lately? It's time. It's time to read a couple of them that you have in your Bible.

GOD IN THE E-MAIL

Many are the plans in a man's heart, but it is the Lord's purpose that prevails.

—Proverbs 19:21

I get e-mails from teachers, friends, preachers, news sources, and from kids. Usually when I get an e-mail from one of my own kids it has been forwarded a dozen times, sometimes with one hundred or more names attached to it from previous forwarding.

I received a multi-forwarded e-mail from my daughter Kristin when she was in the sixth grade. It came with the usual long list of addresses. The names in the most recent forwards were other sixth-grade girls I recognized as my daughter's friends. I was glad to see all their names on this e-mail. I was glad to see they thought this was worth forwarding on! I hope they all read it. The letter was short but pretty insightful. I don't know who wrote it, but I thank all these sixth graders for passing it around until it finally got to my computer. Here is the e-mail:

If God brings you to it, he will bring you through it.

Happy moments, praise God.
Difficult moments, seek God.
Quiet moments, worship God.
Painful moments, trust God.
Every moment, thank God.

It is a short but theologically profound message. "Many are the plans in a man's heart, but it is the Lord's purpose that prevails." We have our plans. We formulate our dreams. We set our goals. We determine our purpose. But there is a bigger purpose for our lives, one that can frustrate our selfish plans, dreams, and goals, or one that can expand them beyond anything we ever imagined. That is the purpose God has for us.

I have two friends who came from wealthy families that owned their own successful businesses. Both of these young men had their purpose in life planned for them by someone else—to return home after college to work in the family business. But both men had decided on a different course for their lives—ministry. Both men were led to Christ while in college, both were led by God to reconsider their futures, and both turned down lucrative offers back home to pursue full-time ministry. They both experienced the happy, difficult, quiet, and painful moments that the poem above refers to. But through it all, both men felt the purpose of God for their lives, and they sought him. Their purpose became praising, seeking, worshiping, and trusting God. "In every moment, thank God."

"Many are the plans in a man's heart, but it is the Lord's purpose that prevails."

I don't know if the sixth graders passing this e-mail around realize the full significance of what they are forwarding. But I hope they keep this message and read it often through the years. Right now and in their future, they will be tested. Their faith will be tested, their goals will be tested, their morality will be tested, and their purpose in life will be tested. I hope they remember that "in every moment, thank God," and "many are the plans in a man's heart, but it is the Lord's purpose that prevails." Because no matter what our purpose, God's purpose is the one that will ultimately prevail.

I hope we are sensitive to God's tug in our lives and we give ourselves to his will. When his plans become our plans, we are functioning in God's purpose and we are emboldened with God's presence in our lives.

A BANGED-UP LIFE

If you falter in times of trouble, how small is your strength!
—Proverbs 24:10

A beginning writer submits eleven manuscripts for publication. All eleven are rejected. Not one editor even offered hope to the young writer that he would ever measure up and see any of his words in print.

A teenager can't resist the pressure from her friends to just show up at the party even if she doesn't "do anything." "Just hang around and have some fun." She does and never once lowers her standard to do some of the things she sees going on. Still some of the kids there can't resist the pleasure of tarnishing the girl's name by spreading false stories.

A new Christian makes himself vulnerable. He preaches his first sermon when the preacher is away. He thinks everything went fine until a well-intentioned member informs him he misquoted two verses and mispronounced three words.

To any number of people, these three are failures. They tried and failed. They suffered rejection, a besmirched name, and public mistakes. Each one of them hurt.

One young preacher was excited about preaching his first sermon. He thought he did well until a well-intentioned member caught him afterward. "How do you know there were three wise men? If you are going to tell stories from the Bible you better get them straight!" The young preacher was so devastated he almost gave up—almost quit, never to preach again. But despite the discouragement, he didn't quit. He hung in there and became a great preacher and teacher of preachers.

We are only failures if we think we are. It doesn't matter what an editor says, some gossipy peers, or a flagrant critic. What goes on in our own minds? What do we tell ourselves? What will we believe? Even more important than these self-questions is this: what does God say?

God is in the business of taking rejected writers, ostracized teens, and struggling preachers and saying, "It's okay. I've got a place for you." In fact, God makes room for addicts, adulterers, liars, thieves, idolaters, homosexuals, and others. "And that is what some of you were. But you were washed, you were sanctified, you were justified in the name of the Lord Jesus Christ and by the Spirit of our God" (1 Cor. 6:11).

New life is found in Jesus Christ. So is ultimate fulfillment. The criticisms and rejections of others don't have the final word about our value, and we shouldn't let them. God has something else to say about us.

One of my favorite scenes in the movie Seabiscuit is where the horse trainer, Tom Smith, is sitting by a campfire. Just off from the fire is a white horse that Tom is doctoring for a bad leg. The future owner of Seabiscuit comes up and asks, "What are you taking care of that horse for?" Tom acts like that is a ridiculous question. He says, "You know, you don't throw a whole life away just because it's banged up a little." Later, the owner gets to turn that statement back on Tom. Tom is upset because Seabiscuit lost a race due to mishandling by the jockey, Johnny. Johnny is blind in his right eye and can't see a horse coming up on that side. When Tom wants to fire the jockey for lying, Seabiscuit's owner says, "Tom, you don't throw a whole life away just because it's banged up a little."

That is what 1 Corinthians 6:11 says. "Bad leg? Blind in one eye? Moral indiscretion? A lie? Rejection? Alone? Have you faltered in times of trouble? Well, I'm not the kind of God who throws a whole life away just because you are banged up a little. In your time of trouble, I will be your strength."

GETTING EVEN

Do not say, "I'll do to him as he has done to me; I'll pay that man back for what he did."

—Proverbs 24:29

There is something about revenge that is sweet. The whole idea of getting even, of making someone hurt the way they made us hurt, is tantalizing. Can't you imagine someone sitting comfortably in a chair, smiling with anticipation at the prospect of making someone else uncomfortable? Maybe you can imagine it because maybe you have done that?

Revenge is so sweet that often times when we get revenge, we don't just get even. No, we go the extra mile and make the rascals who hurt us hurt even more. The longer we hold onto our hurts and nurture the idea of getting even, the more the negative emotions brew inside of us. They stew. They gurgle and boil over, like that feeling of a sour stomach just troubling to explode. Not a very pleasant image, is it? Neither is revenge.

So when the opportunity comes along to expel those negative emotions, those sour attitudes, it's hard to just stop at the point of getting even. How do you cap a volcano? How do you tell a soured stomach to just calm down? Once the action starts, just get out of the way! After days, months, even years of fomenting a spirit of revenge, you don't just cap it. You don't just calm it down. When it starts to explode, someone is going to get hurt, and it may not be just the people at whom you have been angry. Vengeful explosions spew on everyone within reach of the foul discharge!

Remember Absalom? He was certainly justified in wanting to see his poor sister get justice. David was certainly wrong in ignoring the travesty committed against Tamar. For months Absalom stewed. Finally, there was an explosion, an explosion so far-reaching that two brothers ended up dead and a kingdom ended up temporarily divided.

It is intriguing to think that it might have been Absalom's half brother Solomon who wrote, "Do not say, I'll do to him as he has done to me; I'll pay that man back for what he did" (Proverbs 24:29. This verse appears in a section of Proverbs entitled Further Sayings of the Wise, so Solomon may not have been the author). Is the author of this verse writing from personal experience? If it was Solomon, what did he learn from seeing the anger in his own family, from watching brother killing brother, son trying to kill the father, a brother killed in his own rebellion? Maybe Solomon learned, "It's not good to say, I'll do to him as he has done to me. I'll pay that man back for what he did" from the tragic experiences of his home.

There has to be a better way of processing hurt and injustice than storing up bitterness and anger for future explosions. A glimpse into the heart of Jesus reveals such a way: Love your enemies and pray for those who persecute you . . . Forgive men when they sin against you . . . Forgive your brother from your heart . . . Bless those who curse you . . . Do to others as you would have them do to you . . . Be merciful, just as your Father is merciful.

I've learned that vengeance is hard work. It takes time and energy. It can consume days, even years, of your life in plotting and scheming. It makes sense to put that same amount of time and energy into loving actions that promote healing and reconciliation.

SECOND FIDDLE

Do not exalt yourself in the king's presence, and do not claim a place among great men.

—Proverbs 25:6

A conductor for an orchestra was asked, "What is the hardest position to fill?" His answer: "Second fiddle." I understand that the job of second fiddle is to make the first chair look good. No one stands and applauds for second chair. It is not a position where one is exalted, either by self or others. Second fiddle is always in service to the first chair.

Not everyone can play second fiddle, but thank God for those who can. Do you know any second-fiddle people? There is one in the Bible—Andrew. Andrew was one of the first disciples to meet Jesus. He was first a follower of John the Baptist. Jesus came along, and John said, "Look, the Lamb of God" (John 1:36). That was all John had to say. Andrew and another disciple took off to follow Jesus.

There are three important stories in the Bible about Andrew. In the first story Andrew met Jesus and spent the day with him. He was so excited about being with Jesus he had to run and tell someone. Do you know whom he told? His brother Simon Peter. "Hey Simon, come on, we have met the Christ!" (John 1:35–42).

In the second story Jesus was preaching to a group of about five thousand men. Jesus wanted to feed them when they got hungry. When Philip complained that it would take eight months of a man's salary to feed that crowd, Jesus wasn't deterred. "Is there any food here at all?" There was a boy there with five loaves of bread and two fishes. Guess who found that boy and took him to Jesus? It was Andrew. With that food Jesus performed a miracle that fed everyone (John 6:5–13).

In the third story some Greeks came to see Jesus. We don't know why they came to see him, and the disciples didn't know either. When the Greeks told Philip they wanted to speak to Jesus, Philip didn't know what to do. He went to Andrew and said, "Hey, these Gentiles want to see Jesus!" Andrew didn't have to wonder what to do. He said, "Come with me, guys" and took them to meet Jesus (John 12:20–22).

In all three of these stories, Andrew did something very important—he took people to meet Jesus. First, he took a member of his own family. Then he took a young boy. Then he took some strangers. Not only were they strangers, but they were Greeks, Gentiles.

You know what is interesting in all this? Andrew never became one of the more prominent apostles. He was the first to meet Jesus and one of the first to begin following, but his name never made it up in lights. He never became a part of the inner circle. But I don't think he cared. Drawing attention to himself was not something Andrew was after.

A shy young boy wanted a role in the school play. His mother feared that he wouldn't win a good role, that it would go to someone more confident and outgoing. On the day of tryouts, the mom went to school to pick up her son. She was prepared for the worst—a sad, distraught little boy who was very disappointed. She was happy to see her son come running out, smiling. "Guess what, Mom! I'm in the play! I've been chosen to clap and cheer!"

It is not our purpose to exalt ourselves in the presence of the king or to occupy a seat among great men. Sometimes in life the role we get to play is second fiddle: to make others look good and to clap and cheer for them. Don't begrudge that role. Such was Andrew's calling and may be ours as well. God may have an important purpose for us to play in the second chair.

WICKED FLEE

The wicked man flees though no one pursues, but the righteous are as bold as a lion.

—Proverbs 28:1

There is a time to flee, and there are some things to flee from. First Corinthians 6:18 says Christians should flee from sexual immorality. Christians are commanded to flee from idolatry (1 Cor. 10:14). First Timothy 6:11 counsels fleeing from materialism or a concern for the "things" of this world. In 2 Timothy 2:22 Paul encourages the young preacher Timothy to flee the evil desires of youth, probably a reference to the misuse of one's time and energy, such as in quarreling, arguing, and fighting.

Joseph was a handsome young man in the service of the Egyptian official, Potiphar. Mrs. Potiphar, the wife of Joseph's master, tried to "exert" her influence on him. Joseph knew there was a time to question. He knew there was a time to argue one's position. But he also knew there was a time to flee.

With Mrs. Potiphar making bold advances on the handsome young teenager, Joseph knew it was time to flee. Leaving his cloak in Mrs. Potiphar's clutches, Joseph fled. Literally, he ran away, fleeing from sexual immorality.

There are instructions for righteous people in numerous places in the Bible telling them there is a time to cut and run. There are times when it is appropriate to flee.

Proverbs 28:1 is not about the righteous fleeing from danger or sin. It is about the unrighteous fleeing from nothing. There is nothing to flee from but their own imaginations. There is a word for people who see danger where there is none, people who flee in fear when there is nothing to fear. The word is paranoid.

Paranoia isn't funny. It is the spiritual and emotional condition of a person who is guilty and ashamed of behavior they don't want anyone to find out about. Their sin was committed in the past but still lives on and controls their present. They continue to be embarrassed and ashamed, fearing everyone knows or will find out about their indiscretions. (Note: paranoia can also be caused by things that were done to us and over which we had no control, such as abuse. I am not discussing these sufferers of paranoia here).

In the Western movies the gunfighters would never sit with their backs to the door. They were always leery of who might come walking in. Paranoia. I've eaten in restaurants with guys who would always insist on a chair where they would be facing the door. "What's the big deal?" I'd ask. "Oh, goes back to my drinking days. I'd never know who might come walking through the door of that bar that might be mad at me from the last fight. I need to be able to see him when he comes in." Years later they are still facing the door, still fleeing though no one is pursuing. Here is how one man described his paranoia:

> There is the deep shame that . . . addicts live with daily. I felt like such a hypocrite when I would go to church. I always had a nagging feeling that people in church somehow knew what I was doing in secret. (Steve Gallagher, At the Altar of Sexual Idolatry [Dry Ridge, KY: Pure Life Ministries, 2000], p. 31)

This is not a good way to live! It doesn't have to be the way we live.

There is a remedy: confession and repentance. Acts 3:19 says, "Repent, then, and turn to God, so that your sins may be wiped out, that times of refreshing may come from the Lord." What is that refreshing? Knowing you are saved, for one. Feeling saved, for another. Of his later saved condition, Steve Gallagher said, "When I finally began walking in victory, it was liberating to be able to look people right in the eye, knowing I had nothing to hide" (p. 31). The Sage describes this man in the second half of his verse: "the righteous are as bold as a lion."

Keep silent about past sin and you'll keep fleeing dangers that aren't there or you'll keep fleeing exposure of sin that is there. But offer up confession and repentance to God, and enjoy the refreshment that can make the paranoid man bold and confident.

TROPHIES

He who conceals his sins does not prosper, but whoever confesses and renounces them finds mercy.

—Proverbs 28:13

David expresses a similar idea as the Sage: "When I kept silent, my bones wasted away through my groaning all day long. For day and night your hand was heavy upon me; my strength was sapped as in the heat of summer" (Ps. 32:3–4).

When I do something really good, I want everyone to know. I want to shout it from the rooftops. I realize it is not good to toot your own horn too much. However, I don't mind if someone else does it for me. "Hey, he scored the winning basket! He kicked the winning goal!" Okay, so nobody really gets to say that about me, but you get my point.

Accomplishments we are proud of we wear as badges of honor. That is why people have plaques and trophies of prior successes adorning their offices. Honors we have received, recognition for contributions to the community, years of service rendered to a club or business, offices held, and championships won are memorialized in our plaques and trophies.

I have a trophy of a baseball team I coached in 1995. It was the Cody, Wyoming Pinnacle Bank Rockies. The first year was a tough building year. But in year two we won the standings championship, going thirteen and two for the season. The league gave Pinnacle Bank, our sponsor, an impressive trophy. I took it to the president of the bank and he said, "Warren, we'll display it for a few weeks and then why don't you take it?" I didn't argue with him, and fourteen years later that trophy is still hanging around. Actually, it is prominently displayed in my office.

We proudly display plaques, trophies, and awards of our successes. It seems we want to be reminded that one time we were recognized for something good we did. Even with the accumulated problems of life that hang around our neck like a noose, we can still look back at that time, that event, and remember that we were part of something good.

But you know, I've never seen anyone with an award honoring a person's failure. "Oh, that plaque? That recognizes the first time I experimented with illegal drugs. That one I got for my second DUI. Cost me a lot money, too. This one over here? I was awarded this trophy for repeatedly lying to my parents. This certificate here is for sexual indiscretions committed in my youth, and this medallion I received from the judge after my second conviction for shoplifting. Yes, sir, these plaques in my office sure tell a story, don't they?"

"When I kept silent, my bones wasted away." I really don't recommend hanging plaques on our walls to call attention to all of our sins and indiscretions, and I don't think David does either. But I do think David says that being open and honest with our sins is the only way to purge our lives of them.

Years later, Paul wrote, "Have nothing to do with the fruitless deeds of darkness, but rather expose them. For it is shameful even to mention what the disobedient do in secret. But everything exposed by the light becomes visible" (Ephesians 5:11–13). I think what exposing to the light means is confession: bringing everything before God, bringing everything out in the open, letting him know and not trying to hide anything.

Displaying trophies of successes cannot erase the memories of failures. No one is fooled by them anyway. I know and you know that a wall of certificates does not eliminate a life of poor judgment, moral lapses, and sinful choices. Only confession can do that. Keep silent, and your bones will waste away as God's heavy hand rests upon you, sapping you of strength and vitality.

So keep your trophies. But keep your honesty, too. Be ready and willing to confess. Be as open with your failures as with your successes, and God's healing hand will be upon you.

CONFESSION

He who conceals his sins does not prosper, but whoever confesses and renounces them finds mercy.

—Proverbs 28:13

You've heard the saying, "Confession is good for the soul." I've seen numerous cases of families wracked from dysfunctional behavior. It might be alcohol, drugs, sex, or gambling that is destroying it from within. Any one of these activities is enough to turn a family upside down and shake all the good right out of it.

A child raised in an environment with these kinds of dysfunctional behaviors will likely experience low self-esteem, poor judgment, risky choices, and resentment. Resentment is often against Mom and Dad for engaging in these kinds of behaviors or for allowing them to go on in the home by one of the kids.

Suppose now that after ten years of such behavior, Mom, Dad, and the kids go in for counseling together. Each one gets to share with the others what they see as the problems. The parents talk to each other and then to the kids. The kids talk to each other and then to the parents. There is a tremendous openness about the destructive behaviors and attitudes of the last decade. Tempers flare. Emotions run wild. Accusations are thrown around the room. Denials ensue. Defenses are up. Boxes of tissue are used. It looks like things could erupt into a volcano of human violence at any moment. Until . . .

Until one person in that family has the heart to say . . . "I'm sorry."

Maybe it is the father who breaks the cycle of denial and verbal violence with the confession, "I'm sorry, honey. I was addicted to my job. I was never home. You had the job of raising three rambunctious boys all by yourself. I missed all their games and all their school programs. I cheated them, you, and myself. And now, here we are in counseling to try to get it straightened out. I see now that it has to start with me. I'm sorry."

Perhaps it is one of the kids who starts this confessional and healing process. "Mom and Dad, I'm sorry. I know I shouldn't have started shoplifting. But we couldn't afford some of the things other kids at school have, and this was the only way I knew to get it. I know this has hurt me and embarrassed you. I'll pay everything back that I can. I'll try to straighten out. And I really am sorry."

"He who conceals his sins does not prosper, but whoever confesses and renounces them finds mercy."

It's as close to a miracle as anything you could hope to see. "I'm sorry." That phrase, offered humbly and sincerely, can diffuse the most volcanic of situations. Anger dissipates and the warmth of forgiveness can begin to flow. Marriages are saved and families are kept intact when one party can be the first to offer a genuine "I'm sorry." I've seen it happen.

It can happen in your home, too.

Solomon's father, David, said that confession brings forgiveness from the Father. "I said, 'I will confess my transgressions to the Lord'—and you forgave the guilt of my sin" (Ps. 32:5). I think this may be the verse that spawned the phrase I used earlier: "Confession is good for the soul."

Confession brings forgiveness from people, too. Forgiveness is one of the blessings God grants a sincere "I'm sorry."

DISCIPLINE

PEOPLE DO NOT HAVE FINANCIAL PROBLEMS

> Honor the Lord with your wealth, with the firstfruits of your crops; then your barns will be filled to overflowing, and your vats will brim over with new wine.
>
> —Proverbs 3:9–10

The title of this essay may have you laughing and thinking, "Wrong! I've had a financial problem for years!" The title is actually part of a quote by Duane Sheriff, which reads, "People at large do not have a financial problem; they have a stewardship, discipline and faithfulness problem."

Duane's comment appears in the book The Storehouse Principle: A Revolutionary God Idea for Creating Extraordinary Financial Stability (Boulder: Cross Staff Publishers, p. 160) by Al Jandl and Van Crouch. The premise of the book is based upon Deuteronomy 28:8: "The Lord will send a blessing on your barns and on everything you put your hand to. The Lord your God will bless you in the land he is giving you."

When God led the Israelites into the Promised Land, he blessed them with homes, fertile fields, and fruit trees. All of their material needs were met. However, God expected faithfulness and obedience from the Israelites. One area where their trust would be tested would be in the rest God demanded for the land. Every seven years the land was to lie fallow. Nothing could be planted. Just as the people and animals received rest every seven days, the land would receive rest every seven years.

What would people eat during that year of rest when the land would not produce food? The food grown in the sixth year would be eaten then, and the extra food that God provided would be saved in a storehouse to eat during the seventh year and then into the eighth year when the people planted crops and waited for the harvest. The crops grown in year six would actually provide food for part of three years.

Would the people trust God so completely that they would not plant their crops and would allow the land to lie at rest? Would they obey God? That was a great test! At least three spiritual attitudes would be necessary for the people to obey. They would need to be faithful. They would need to trust God and obey him whether it made sense to them or not! Secondly, they would need stewardship, meaning they would need to manage their resources (food) responsibly. They would need to save food from year six to carry them through year seven and into year eight. Finally, they would need to practice discipline. No matter how tempted they might be to skimp on what they set aside or to dip into their reserves of food, they had to resist and practice restraint! Enough food had to be set aside to span three years; and strict faith, stewardship, and discipline had to be exercised.

Drawing on this principle, authors Jandl and Crouch contend that the principle of God blessing the storehouse still applies today. Rather than putting food in our storehouse we deposit money. No matter how pressing our wants, needs, or bills may be, some money must be set aside. When we practice restraint in our spending in order to save, we build a storehouse for the future, which God promises to bless. If we don't save, there is no storehouse for God to increase for us.

Saving in ancient Israel or today requires the same spiritual attitudes of faithfulness, stewardship, and discipline. If we lack these virtues, we will spend everything we make and then pull out credit cards. Our financial world will spiral out of control. We will feel stressed, burdened, and angry. We may think we need to make more money. But repeating what one man who practiced the "storehouse principle" says in the book, "People at large do not have a financial problem; they have a stewardship, discipline and faithfulness problem." Often our financial problems are not that we don't make enough money, but that we are not thankful for what we do have and we don't exercise faith, stewardship, and discipline. The crux of our financial woes is a heart that is not obeying God nor trusting him for our spiritual or material security.

CHALLENGE TO CHARACTER

My son, do not despise the Lord's discipline and do not resent his rebuke.

—Proverbs 3:11

I'll bet that there is a person in your life you can't stand. The very thought of that man or woman makes your skin crawl and your heart beat faster. You may feel your blood pressure rise and your face flush. Your breathing becomes labored. Know what is happening? Your body is going into an attack mode. Your hatred for that person is causing your body to respond to the strong emotion you feel. Your mind reads your emotions and prepares your body for either flight or fight. If opportunity allowed, you would verbally scald that person right in front of everyone present. If you humiliated this despised person, you would smile with glee and satisfaction.

Is there anyone in your life you feel that way about? Is there anyone you would like to see broken and shamed the way they deserve to be for how despicably they have treated you?

Well, think about this: God may have put that person in your life. The person you disdain and would love to harm is possibly in your life because God chose to put him there.

That may sound like a ridiculous suggestion. Why would God put a brash, rude, crude, sarcastic person in our lives? Because God knows we need them. God puts people in our lives to challenge our presumptions about ourselves, to confront our own integrity issues, and to spur our character growth.

If it were left up to us, we would surround ourselves with people who love us, affirm us, praise us, and encourage us at every turn. We would surround ourselves with people who would ignore our faults, justify our character flaws, and excuse our sins. Such people are delightfully pleasant to have as friends! The problem is, if our minds are corrupt and our souls depraved, these friends will never let us know. They will let us die pleasantly in our lostness and alienation from God. Such amiable friends never challenge us to assess our spiritual sickness, to humble ourselves before God or friends, and to confess our sins.

How can God awaken us from our spiritual stupor about ourselves? He has to put someone into our lives who will challenge and push us to examine ourselves and face up to our own disgusting attitudes and behavior. No one can do that for us as effectively as the people we can't stand, our enemies.

Our enemies can teach us about ourselves and help us grow in two ways. One, I've learned that what we can't stand about an enemy, whether a coworker, former friend, or even a family member, is often a reflection of the same poor attitudes or behavior in our own lives. We can't stand in others what we sense in ourselves. It is simply easier to condemn it in another than change it in ourselves.

Secondly, the poor behavior of people we don't like may not be a reflection of our own tendencies. Our angry feelings may be a justified response to their sinful, rude, mocking behavior. They may be angry and contentious with everybody, and no one likes them because their actions are so sorry. Thus, their behavior may not be a reflection of any similar behavior in our own lives. So how can they teach us or help us grow? Who else in our lives provides us with the opportunity to practice patience, love, forbearance, forgiveness, grace, and a host of other virtues that we would rather let lie dormant? God wants us to grow in all these areas. If we simply surround ourselves with people who are affirming of how we already are, we might never cultivate the personality of God in our lives any deeper than what it is right now.

I hate to say it, I hate to even think it, but at least occasionally we need those contentious, bickering personalities to stick their heads into our lives and disrupt our ease. We need them for our own spiritual development. "Who can discern his errors?" David asked (Ps. 19:12). Most of us can't, so we need others to do that for us. With open eyes and sensitive hearts, we might find that our enemy is actually God's means of providing life-giving rebuke and wisdom (Prov. 15:31).

Before you avoid your enemy, run from him, gossip about him, or even verbally blister him, pause for a moment and reflect on how God may be using that person in your life for your own good. The person you dislike the most may be the person with the greatest ability to shape your heart to be more like God's.

STINGRAYS

Guard your heart, for it is the wellspring of life.
—Proverbs 4:23

Steve Irwin was shooting a TV show on the Great Barrier Reef in Australia when he was struck in the heart by a stingray's tail and killed.

Stingrays are normally calm, but they are equipped with a long, pointed tail equipped with sharp spines and poison to ward off sharks.

The kids and I loved to watch Steve's show on TV. We loved the nature scenes, the animals, and even Steve's antics. I am amazed how close he would get to crocodiles and poisonous snakes. I think it was Steve we watched who actually put his face right up to the hole of a poisonous snake. The snake stuck its head out, touched Steve's face, then went back into its hole. I thought the man was extreme, but I admired the courage and calmness he had in the midst of danger.

I think two things contributed to Steve's great success on TV as an expert in dealing with wild, dangerous animals. One, Steve had enthusiasm for what he did. His spirit was infectious. I wanted to see what he would do next, and his showmanship kept me glued to his exploits.

Two, Steve knew the animals and himself. He was more in charge of the situation than it looked on TV. He was careful. He always knew where the lines of danger were and was careful not to let that line be crossed, either by the wild animal or himself.

Except for one time.

I say that with sadness because I liked Steve and his show. I will miss both. I also say it with sadness because what Steve experienced with that stingray we all experience with sin.

With all Steve knew about crocodiles, venomous snakes, humpback whales, stingrays and other dangerous critters, he was killed in a matter of seconds because he crossed the line he was always so careful to avoid. I don't think he meant to cross it. Queensland, Australia, police ruled that Steve did not threaten or intimidate the stingray. Right to the end Steve remained respectful of the animals he worked with and filmed. Nonetheless, a line was crossed.

We know all about lying, stealing, pornography, drunkenness, immorality, laziness, gossip, materialism, violence, envy, anger, and selfishness. We know the attractiveness of the sin and the weakness in our own souls. We know to stay away from the line, the line that separates a close admiration of the sin and the lust in our hearts that prompt us to get closer, closer, closer. Sometimes, like Steve, we just get a little too close.

Stingrays have a sharp, barbed tail loaded with poison. When a stingray strikes a human being, it is generally on the foot or leg. It is painful, but rarely, rarely, ever fatal. But sometimes it is.

When we get too close to sin, we expose more than a foot or a leg to the poison barbs. We expose our hearts.

"Guard your heart, for it is the wellspring of life" (Prov. 4:23).

We guard our hearts because they are so defenseless against the poisoned barbs of cruel speech, burning envy, pretty pictures, and the promises of fun. People we love die because they creep too close to the line of danger. Be careful. Live faithfully. Protect your heart.

ROARING LIONS

Disaster will overtake him [the scoundrel and villain] in an instant;
he will suddenly be destroyed—without remedy.
—Proverbs 6:15

It is unfashionable to talk about the devil today except for Halloween and an occasional joke. But the Bible speaks of the reality of the devil. He is not just a costume, nor is he in any way presented as humorous. The devil is dangerous. He is diabolical—that is, incredibly evil. The word "devil" comes from the Greek word diabolos from which we also get "diabolical." In the Bible the devil is not a creature to make light of nor to caricature.

Just consider 1 Peter 5:8–9. "Be self-controlled and alert. Your enemy the devil prowls around like a roaring lion looking for someone to devour. Resist him, standing firm in the faith, because you know that your brothers throughout the world are undergoing the same kind of sufferings."

Peter took the devil seriously. "Be self-controlled and alert." The very nature of the devil requires our best efforts to resist him. A lack of self-control and awareness invites his attacks. Failure to exercise control and discipline invites him to hurl his energies against us. A moral temptation? Another drink? A rude person that provokes your explosive anger? An opportunity to cheat a friend of $25? What is the chink in your armor? What is it the devil can throw in front of you at a weak moment to hook you and reel you in? There is something in every one of us, some weakness that the devil is ready to exploit. So Peter says, "Be aware. Be on guard. Be disciplined."

Being self-controlled and alert is one line of defense. The second is to resist the devil. Self-control and alertness is a defensive posture. Resisting him means to go on the offensive. The full comment Peter makes is "Resist him, standing firm in the faith." Billboards with racy ads can call to mind an illicit relationship. Friends offering you a substance to relax you can threaten your sobriety. Coworkers who cheat on the job and invite your participation can erode your honesty and threaten your integrity. You didn't ask for any of these inducements to sin, but here they are! You can be self-controlled and alert, but still temptation comes on like a freight train. What do you do now? Fight back, Peter says. Go on the offensive. Resist the devil, stand firm. Exercise the strength God gives you to say no, and refuse to give in.

Anyone who has ever overcome an addiction knows the difficulty of going it alone. That is why there is AA and NA. God knows the difficulty of going it alone in our struggle against sin. So he gives us a community. Peter calls to our remembrance the brothers and sisters we have all around the world that are also doing battle against the evil one. We share this struggle with others.

Interestingly, Peter compares the devil to a hungry lion looking for someone to devour. Have you ever encountered a hungry lion? I might have. Several years ago I was hunting outside Cody, Wyoming. I was up about eight thousand feet in deep snow. My co-hunter, Marion Phillips, was in the pickup, and I walked alone along a ridge. On the sweep back to the truck I was walking close to a wooded area. I heard a growl coming from the forest. My heart beat faster. I readied my rifle. I studied the woods for several minutes. I didn't want to turn my back on it for fear that whatever was growling at me would come after me. I finally started to walk off but heard it again—a clear, distinct growl. Now my heart was really pounding, as I suspected it was a mountain lion making his presence known. I was self-controlled and alert, just like Peter said. I was even prepared for a more aggressive defense—my rifle was shouldered. I was ready to resist an attack. I could feel "disaster" coming upon me!

Fortunately, no attack came. I'm not sure what growled at me that day. I just got out of there in a hurry. But since then 1 Peter 5:8-9 has meant more to me. Lions, the devil, a villainous lifestyle—these are not as apt to hurt you if you are prepared for their attack. You can prepare yourself with alertness, self-control, resistance to evil, and God's presence in your life.

OVERLOAD

> An anxious heart weighs a man down, but a kind word cheers
> him up.
>
> —Proverbs 12:25

Jared exploded. His secretary brought him a reminder that he had a two o'clock meeting with the supervisor and was to present his ideas for the new job his company was working on. She set a note on his desk and said, "Don't forget your meeting this afternoon" before turning to walk out of his office. She was not prepared for what erupted.

Jared exploded out of his chair hurling verbal assaults at the woman who was only doing her job. "Don't you think I can remember a stupid meeting? Do you think I need you riding my case here at work like my wife does at home? I know what I am supposed to be doing. And even if I am late for the meeting and my presentation, don't I do enough around here? The boss can make all the demands he wants, but he won't get any more production out of me because I am doing everything possible to produce around here, something you and the others should start doing!"

The secretary froze in shock and fear. Jared's explosion was so uncharacteristic that she did not know how to process what happened. Jared was generally gentlemanly and kind. What happened? "An anxious heart weighs a man down."

What Jared's secretary, boss, and wife didn't know was that Jared had been on the fast track to some kind of emotional explosion or spiritual meltdown for some time. Every moment of Jared's life was crammed with some kind of activity: teaching classes at church, a fifty-hour workweek, playing on the company softball team, coaching a kids' sports team, volunteering for community projects.

Besides these time constraints on his life, other aspects of Jared's life were suffering. Even though he taught classes at church, he didn't take the time to study, reflect, and pray. He had no devotional time with his wife or family. He spent little personal time with his wife or children in conversation or recreation time. And as is quite typical of young to middle-aged families, the family finances were considerably strained. All of this had been building up in Jared. Over the years the internal pressure rose exponentially. So when the poor secretary very responsibly reminded Jared of the meeting with his boss, she unknowingly popped an over-stressed balloon.

One word might suffice to describe Jared's condition: "overload." According to Richard Swenson, a medical doctor, "Overloading occurs whenever the requirements upon us exceed that which we are able to bear" (Margin: Restoring Emotional, Physical, Financial, And Time Reserves to Overloaded Lives [Colorado Springs, CO: NavPress, 1992], p. 74). Swenson says we all have limits of time, emotions, and performance. When we stretch those limits too far, we overload. Areas of overload our society suffers from include activity, commitment, competition, debt, expectation, fatigue, hurry, information, noise, technology, and work. Overload can cause anxiety, emotional breakdown, hostility, depression, and resentment (pp. 79–87).

Anybody who knew the drains on Jared's emotions, time, and energy would know that he was a volcano waiting to explode. He did explode, just like many people do. Overload is a major reason why. "An anxious heart weighs a man down."

The best antidote to overload is to unload. Be kind to yourself! Commit to fewer things. Cut down on technology use. Slow down. Then, add some positive family—and relaxation-building practices, such as quiet nights at home with your family, reading a book, praying, taking a walk with your spouse and children. Slow down, connect with people, connect with God, feed your spirit. If a kind word can cheer an anxious heart, so can some self-directed kind deeds.

HUNGER OF THE SOUL

Better a little with the fear of the Lord than great wealth with turmoil.
—Proverbs 15:16

I've been blessed with abundance. Only one time was I faced with the prospect of not having food in the cupboard or the money to buy any. Even then though, God provided my graduate school roommate Bobby Lawson and me with Narcissus, a sweet older lady from church with a cupboard full of food that she was willing to share. Narcissus fed us along with many other hungry graduate students.

I've been a day or longer without food, but it has always been by choice or illness. It's never been a matter of not having any food available somewhere. I've never had to wake up to face a second or third day of hunger and praying in earnest that on this day God would help me find work and a meal. Millions of people around the world face this hunger, daily, with no prospect for food.

Mother Teresa gave a hungry little girl on the streets of India a piece of bread. The child ate slowly, crumb by crumb. "Eat, eat the bread. You are hungry," Mother Teresa told the child. "I am afraid," the girl said. "When the bread will be finished, I will be hungry again" (Mother Teresa, No Greater Love [Novato, CA: New World Library, 1997], p. 97). How desperate must be the plight of a homeless child who can't truly enjoy the bread she is eating today without thinking of the despair she will feel tomorrow when hunger invades her body again. Can we imagine anything worse than the gnawing hopelessness of poverty?

The Sage can. "Better a little with the fear of the Lord than great wealth with turmoil." The term "little" may not refer to complete poverty, but it does refer to limited resources. In America we think of even limited resources as being poor. We like abundance! Can any of us get by with only two pairs of dress shoes? How many homes have only one television set anymore? We want leftovers to snack on during the movie. Abundance.

Better than having abundance is to have only a little, even to experience some level of poverty, if you have a relationship with God. To live in fear of the Lord is to know God, experience him, and live in covenant with him. The man who fears God is transforming into the image of God. He lives with character, integrity, and healthy relationships. He has family, friends, community. This is wealth that transcends any earthly abundance we might boast.

Worse than the gnawing hopelessness of material poverty is poverty of the soul. A closet full of suits, a cupboard full of food, and a bank account full of money cannot compensate for the soul that is void of the fear of God. Our souls long for genuine sustenance, value, and fullness. That hunger cannot be fed with anything the hand of man produces. It can only be fed with a sense of God's presence.

> The world today is hungry not only for bread but hungry for love, hungry to be wanted, to be loved. They're hungry to feel the presence of Christ. In many countries, people have everything except that presence, that understanding. In every country there are poor. On certain continents poverty is more spiritual than material, a poverty that consists of loneliness, discouragement, and the lack of meaning in life. (No Greater Love, p. 93–94)

"Turmoil" is a word that describes the life void of God's presence. Instead of peace and contentment, the spiritually empty soul seeks to satiate its hunger with things. It is a vain attempt to find meaning, since it is God alone who gives genuine meaning. "Better a little with the fear of the Lord."

FOLLOW THE RED ROAD

The path of the upright is a highway.
—Proverbs 15:19

I know a young Native American boy who is working to straighten his life out. Drugs and alcohol have messed him up. Possible legal repercussions have convinced him that he needs to turn his life around.

His grandfather is steeped in the old Indian ways. He abhors the careless lifestyle that addiction breeds. He tells his grandson, "Follow the red road."

"What does that mean?" I asked my friend.

"It means 'follow the old Indian ways,'" he said, "the ways of discipline and loyalty to your tribe and people. It means living responsibly."

Follow the red road. Follow the path of the upright. "The path of life leads upward for the wise" (Prov. 15:24).

I like that expression. It speaks of the Indian boy's heritage, the old ways of tribal pride, responsibility, and importance. It speaks of maintaining and upholding the community, family, and individual honor. That is how this boy's grandfather tries to live as he serves the tribe as a leader.

Follow the red road. That is a good saying to express the goal of noble thoughts and aspirations. I can think of a few sayings that achieve that same goal and challenge us to lift our thoughts and aspirations even higher than one's cultural tradition.

Be perfect, therefore, as your heavenly Father is perfect.

Seek first the kingdom of God.

Whatever you do in word or deed, do all in the name of the Lord.

Press on toward the goal to win the prize for which God has called (us).

Set your hearts on things above.

These words all come from the Bible, some of them from Jesus. All of them challenge us to place our allegiance on something higher than ourselves. They challenge us to live lives of noble aspirations, dignity, service to others, and high moral standards.

My young friend has lived a life of carelessness and addiction. He spent his God-given health and talents in wasted efforts and self-destructive behavior. This is certainly not how God wants him to live.

But this boy is changing because he has two things going for him: a grandfather of high moral character who will never give up on him and the Son of God who will never give up on him.

I'd like to say that everything in my friend's life is changing for the right direction: that he is considering college and a career, that he is honoring God in his life, and that he is sober. He will do these good things if he remembers the words of his wise old grandfather: follow the red road. Even better, I hope he remembers the principle from Proverbs that "the path of the upright is a highway."

SELF-CONTROL

Better a patient man than a warrior, a man who controls his temper than one who takes a city.

—Proverbs 16:32

We recognize power. We recognize power in the muscle-laden lineman who plows over his opposition on the football field. We recognize it in a boxer who sends his opponent to the mat with one crushing blow of his right hand. We recognize it in the warrior who overwhelms his enemy and conquers a city.

A warrior who could take a city in ancient times was a feared man. Today, at least in theory, certain brutalities of war are managed by conventions and treaties (although they are not always honored). At least among combatants in the western nations, POWs are not supposed to be abused and killed, civilian sections of a town are not to be razed, and the women are not to be brutalized.

In ancient times there were no such conventions governing the behavior of the conquering warriors. Whatever they found in the conquered city was theirs for the taking. They could help themselves to the gold and silver, artwork, fancy clothing, and the women. Life was horrible for residents in a conquered city. They had no defense or plea. The thought of the invading army seemed to be, "If we are powerful enough to conquer, we are powerful enough to do whatever we want."

God doesn't agree with that. God made provisions in the Old Testament that governed the brutality of the conquering army. Early in her history Israel was ordered to put entire populations to the sword because their lifestyles were so sinful. But as the nation of Israel was settled, the troops of Israel were placed under certain restrictions. For example, women of the conquered region were to be afforded more gentle care than they would have received from other armies (see Deut. 20:10–14).

Our power does not impress God, and it certainly does not give us liberty to abuse and misuse other people. Physical power is deceptive. It is intoxicating. It makes one think they have license to satisfy any craving, any lust, any want they have. If they are powerful enough to take and use, they are powerful enough to have and enjoy.

But that isn't real strength. That explosion of selfish energy actually reveals weakness, an internal weakness where the locus of power is really exercised. Beating a conquered POW and taking his wife for your own isn't power, it is an abuse of power. It is a lack of internal control. "Better a patient man than a warrior, a man who controls his temper than one who takes a city."

God views strength as the quality of self-control and restraint. All through the Bible God counsels against taking and having something just because we want it. The Ten Commandments tell us not to covet and take something that isn't ours, whether a neighbor's house, animal, or wife. Even if we can take it, we don't. In the New Testament the man deemed worthy of leading God's people is not the man who gives vent to his passions and explodes in anger and hostility (1 Tim. 3:2–3). His violence may seem like an expression of power, and he will certainly scare his wife and kids with his outbursts; but that does not make him a powerful man. He is weak and out of control. He may take a city or at least scare his family, but lack of patience and self-control actually renders him very weak.

"Better a patient man than a warrior, a man who controls his temper than one who takes a city." At the heart of this proverb is the idea that one with self-control demonstrates more power than one who can control others through fear, brutality, or physical strength. Self-control is not easy, but it is possible with God's presence in our lives.

WORDS ARE POWERFUL

The tongue has the power of life and death.
—Proverbs 18:21

Jake raced around the end of the defenders to get outside for the pass. His ten-year-old legs didn't get him there fast enough, and the play collapsed. "That was the worst running I've ever seen," the quarterback said to him with a smile.

The smile was supposed to let Jake know it was a joke. Jake looked up at the quarterback, his youth minister. He may have seen the smile, but it didn't offset the piercing words that wound around his heart and crushed it. Jake felt the power of death.

Words have power. People in tribal communities that believe in demons and spirits will prosper or die based on the words of their local holy man. Whether or not the spirit actually administers the death is immaterial. The fact that people believe in the words imbue them with the power to move and act. People live or die on the power of words.

Jesus used words to grant life, offer hope, and open up new possibilities for meaning. Heaven itself clothed his words with force. "The first shall be last and the last shall be first." These words planted in the ground of fertile hearts produce servants who pour their lives out in service to God and neighbors. How could Stephen possibly pray for his executioners, "Lord, do not hold this sin against them"? The words of Jesus for his murderers reverberate in all hearts that have heard them: "Father, forgive them, for they do not know what they are doing." Men find strength to forgive because the words of forgiveness offered by Jesus still resonate with possibility. Marriages are saved, friendships restored, and churches unified because the words of Jesus empower them to serve and forgive.

"The tongue has the power of life and death." With our speech we can extend hope to a man on death row or we can crush the life of a little boy. In our mouths we carry life and death, hope or defeat, heaven or hell. "The mouth of the righteous is a fountain of life, but violence overwhelms the mouth of the wicked" (Prov. 10:11).

Too little thought is given to the effect our words have or the life they take after they flow from our mouths. Our words can be refreshing water to the thirsty in spirit, or they can produce violence that overwhelms the speaker and his victim. When David said, "Get her for me," was he giving any thought to the eruption of violence his words had birthed?

Words are performative. They cause things to happen. Words bring a smile to a face or a tear to an eye. They draw people to our hearts or they drive them away. They generate appreciation or ignite burning resentment. Words offer life or sentence to death.

When the women went to the tomb they were met by an angel who said, "He has risen . . . go tell the disciples 'he has risen.'" These three words have been performing for two thousand years. Every time we repeat them, we create new possibilities for people to lift up their heads and see what God has to offer them. These are the words of life, hope, and eternity.

Perhaps not every word carries the weight of "Father, forgive them" or "He has risen," but our words do inspire or discourage. No word should be spoken carelessly or thoughtlessly because of the immense hurt and damage it can cause. Lying, gossiping, complaining, and criticizing do not inspire life for the recipient or the speaker. Take to heart Jesus' warning to us: "I tell you that men will have to give account on the day of judgment for every careless word they have spoken" (Matt. 12:36). Flavor your words with love and grace, so they can inspire "the power of life" to you and to the one who hears them.

DEBT SLAVERY

> The rich rule over the poor, and the borrower is servant to the lender.
>
> —Proverbs 22:7

To be a servant to someone means you are in their employ. In some contexts the term servant can be demeaning. The term may indicate more than just being employed by someone; it can mean you are under their control. If you are someone's employee, you can just quit if you want to. But if you are a servant to them, you may be deeper in their grasp and not free to quit. This word for servant can also be used for a slave.

I think that is the idea the Sage has here. If you owe money to a bank or a finance company, you can't just quit your "relationship" with them. You are a servant to them. You are in bondage. You can't walk away from the money you owe. You must pay it off. "The borrower is servant to the lender."

The Message by Eugene Peterson captures this idea with greater clarity. "The poor are always ruled over by the rich, so don't borrow and put yourself under their power" (Colorado Springs: NavPress Publishing, 1996). If debt is so binding, so demeaning, so slave making, why do we let ourselves get so mired in it? Dave Ramsey explains:

> Debt is so ingrained into our culture that most Americans can't even envision a car without a payment, a house without a mortgage, a student without a loan, and credit without a card. We have been sold debt with such repetition and with such fervor that most folks cannot conceive what it would be like to have no payments. Just as slaves born into slavery can't visualize freedom, we Americans don't know what it would be like to wake up to no debt. (Dave Ramsey, The Total Money Makeover [Nashville: Thomas Nelson, 2003], p. 19)

For many of us, servicing four, five, or six different debt payments is as common and acceptable as eating out every Sunday. In fact, it is likely that we'll charge the Sunday meal to our growing credit-card debt and pay it off over the next several months! Debt is an accepted and expected way of life. If you want to challenge that statement, just tell some of your friends that you have definite plans to get out and stay out of debt. Be prepared for some ridicule.

Ramsey continues:

> I have found that a major barrier to winning (over debt) is our view of debt. Most people who have made the decision to stop borrowing money have experienced something weird: ridicule. Friends and family who are disciples of the myth that debt is good have ridiculed those on the path to freedom. (Ramsey, p. 19)

If you owe very much money, you know the emotions of slavery: feeling trapped, experiencing desperation as you worry about getting financially free, fearing college costs for your children, dreading retirement, lying awake at night as visions of credit cards dance through your head, buying into moneymaking schemes, arguing with your spouse, and getting short with your kids. "The borrower is servant to the lender."

You don't have to stay a debt slave. Ramsey not only rages against debt; he teaches the way out of it. I recommend his book and his thirteen-week class. Debt slavery is self-imposed; freedom from debt is achieved through self-discipline. With some determination and hard work, we can all wave good-bye to the lender, break the chains of debt slavery, and enjoy financial and emotional freedom.

DEBT FREEDOM

The rich rule over the poor, and the borrower is servant to the lender.
—Proverbs 22:7

Do not be a man who strikes hands in pledge or puts up security for debts.
—Proverbs 22:26

Debt slavery is depressing. More encouraging is the idea of debt freedom. But we are unlikely to do the work it takes to enjoy debt freedom unless we have first felt the pain of debt slavery. Here is a little pain before we move on to freedom.

Did you know that one of our nation's founding fathers wrote about debt slavery? Here are some gems from Benjamin Franklin:

> Think what you do when you run in debt; you give to another Power over your Liberty.

> Creditors have better memories than debtors.

> Creditors are a superstitious sect, great observers of set days and times. The day comes around before you are aware, and the demand is made before you are prepared to satisfy it. Or if you bear your debt in mind, the term which at first seemed so long, will, as it lessens, appear extremely short . . . Those have a short Lent who owe money to be paid at Easter.

> Since the borrower is a slave to the lender, and the debtor to the creditor, disdain the chain, preserve your freedom, and maintain your independence: be industrious and free; be frugal and free.

> So rather go to be supperless than rise in debt. (Benjamin Franklin, The Autobiography and Other Writings [New York: Signet Books], pp. 195–96).

Ron Blue, in The Debt Squeeze: How Your Family Can Become Financially Free (Pomona, CA: Focus on the Family, 1989), says there are four common causes of debt. The first is a lack of discipline. Being self-disciplined means making the right decisions about money, spending and saving consistently. Lack of discipline in these areas means getting into debt and financial slavery. The second reason is a lack of contentment, simply not being happy and grateful for what we already have. Thirdly, a search for security lures people into spending money they don't have. As Christians we have no reason to acquire for the sake of security because Christ meets our deepest needs. Finally, people get into debt in a vain search for significance. To many of us, owning some special "thing" makes us somebody (pp. 10–19).

Are you tired of the pain of debt? Do you want to get out? You can. To begin, Ron says we need to take personal responsibility for the financial situation we are in. We are responsible for our decisions, our choices, and our spending. "Only when you and I take personal responsibility for going into debt can we hope to start working our way out of it" (p. 24).

How do we get out of debt? "You get out of debt little by little over time, and the major requirement is discipline" (p. 56). Ron gives four simple steps. While the steps seem simple, it is difficult to make the decision to climb out, to be disciplined over time, and to keep our eyes focused to the end.

First, determine where you are. Know your total amount of debt. That figure may shock and scare you! Secondly, stop going into debt. Simply refuse to borrow more or charge more. Thirdly, develop a repayment plan. You may need to sell some of your possessions, raid your savings account, and reduce your living expenses. You'll need a budget for this. Finally, establish accountability with someone you trust (pp. 55–69).

Too many Christians live in the vice of debt. We can be free. Books like the one by Ron Blue and Dave Ramsey can help move us from debt slavery to debt freedom.

WORK AND HOUSES

> Finish your outdoor work and get your fields ready; after that, build your house.
>
> —Proverbs 24:27

After four years of college, three years of law school, and two summers of interning, the young lawyer has his first real job. He has a good salary, benefits, and money that will be put away for retirement. Everything is in place for his life. After all of his hard work and discipline, it seems as though he has arrived.

What is next? To be a professional he has to look like one, so he needs the clothes, expensive ones that "make the man." He needs a car that will appropriately reflect on his new status. He needs a membership in the country club. The price tag for a house near the country club is high, but he will be getting raises that will cover all these purchases, he figures.

What the young lawyer doesn't anticipate is that he will also have to work eighty hours a week to pay for his purchases. He will find it hard to be involved with church and build a close family life under these kinds of working conditions. Only after experiencing these things will he realize the wisdom of Proverbs: "Finish your outdoor work and get your fields ready; after that, build your house."

This proverb uses imagery of a farmer's obligations. The farmer needs a house to live in and pays for his house with income generated from labor on the land. Putting things in the appropriate order, the farmer must labor then build, work then enjoy, toil then rest. Everything in its proper order.

This wisdom is not for the farmer alone. The wisdom of the sages often has application beyond its immediate context. Couldn't all of us benefit from applying ourselves to work, practicing thrift and saving money, and then enjoying the benefits of our blessings?

Shortly after Cheryl and I were married, we had a visit from some long-time friends who were the age of our parents. The man told us about experiences he had trying to hire some recent college graduates.

"You know, these young people graduate college, look for employment, and expect to get paid top dollar right from the start. An entry-level position is something their parents had to endure. They want to start in management. Then they want a new car and a house like their parents have. They don't realize their mom and dad had to work and save for twenty-five years to get what they have now. This generation wants it from the start." "Finish your outdoor work and get your fields ready; after that, build your house."

Microwave ovens and remote-control TV's generate an unspoken expectation in us that everything in our lives ought to be instant. We want instant food and an instant channel change, so doesn't it follow that we should have instant success, instant financial boon, and instant creature comforts, like expensive cars and houses? Why not? Even if the high salary doesn't follow immediately on the heels of college graduation, credit makes everything possible. Our motto today could be, "Build your house first, and get the car, the stereo system and the nice clothes; after that, work your job, pay the bills and save some money."

Instant gratification does not guarantee long-term satisfaction. The wise person, the one who looks at his long-range plans for life, establishes priorities, sets goals, and disciplines himself to do his work. Gradually, as some level of success is achieved, he buys his house. No, not the one that will be the rave of his peer group, but a house that will reflect his modest level of success. The wise man knows there are still more fields to plow and seeds to sow before he enjoys the fruit of his labor too much.

WHAT DO YOU DO WITH YOUR ANGER?

Anger is cruel and fury overwhelming.
—Proverbs 27:4

While you're driving to work one morning, a car pulls right out in front of you, causing you to slam on your brakes. Your coffee sloshes out of the cup spilling all over your clothes. Work papers on the car seat are strewn all over the floorboard. Your anger surges and your heart leaps into overdrive! You cast an accusatory glance at the offending driver and motor on. Over the next few moments, your anger dissipates.

Consider the same scenario again. A driver pulls out in front of you, causing you to slam on the brakes, splash your coffee, scatter your papers, and race your heart. You are angry. But this time you don't just cast an accusing glance and then drive on. You curse, you make obscene gestures, and you harass the other driver. You drive beside him, staring angrily and blasting out obscenities. Eventually your cars separate, but your anger does not gradually dissipate. Instead, it lingers. It even grows, taking on a life of its own. Even at the office you bubble over with hostility, taking out your anger on coworkers, blasting them with belittling remarks. Your whole day is consumed with this inner hostility that goes way beyond the provocation that a careless driver caused. You are seething with an anger that comes from deep, deep within your being.

This kind of deep-seated anger travels in two directions. It travels back in time, back to before you can even remember. Slights you suffered as a child, neglect from your parents, ostracism from your peer group, the feeling of being abandoned and struggling under demands you could not live up to may all be contributing to your current anger. So when that driver pulled out in front of your car, you weren't just responding to that driver. You were responding to years of perceived abuse and put-downs that have been driving you for years.

This kind of anger also travels within you. Anger is embedded deeply within your psyche. Your unconscious memory bank is bursting with incidents from your past that you have managed to suppress. Your consciousness is overflowing with painful memories that you are all too ready to call into service to spew anger. Your conscience is scarred with guilt because of the times you have let your anger burn someone else. Shame is crammed in there too. This kind of anger is deeply suppressed and embedded in every fiber of your being. It causes you to lash out at injustices both real and imagined. It erodes your insides, causing depression. This is real anger. What do you do with it?

First, admit it. Even if you don't know all the specific incidents that make up your state of anger, you can recognize that you are an angry person. Your depression and sudden eruptions are telltale signs of your anger.

Secondly, identify it. Why are you angry? Neglected as a kid? Failure to live up to expectations? Is your anger your fault?

Thirdly, confess and repent of your anger. Ultimately, the anger you are carrying in your heart and mind, the anger that you mask with a false sweetness after ugly outbursts, the anger that causes you to doubt yourself and intimidate others to compensate for your sense of smallness . . . ultimately, this anger is your responsibility. It is wrong. So confess it and repent of it.

Finally, forgive. Forgive your parents if they were neglectful or required more of you than you were able to deliver. Forgive your brothers or sisters if they were unkind siblings. Forgive yourself if you failed. Seek God's forgiveness. "If you forgive men when they sin against you, your heavenly Father will also forgive you" (Matt. 6:14). Let go of that anger.

STRAYING FROM HOME

Like a bird that strays from its nest is a man who strays from his home.
—Proverbs 27:8

What is it like for a bird that strays from its nest? I grew up on a farm in the country. We had trees all around our house with birds' nests in them. Occasionally we would find a baby bird on the ground below the nest. I wondered if the bird was sick and the mother had to push it out. Maybe the bird was rambunctious and tried taking off from home before it was capable of flying. Did it fall to its death because it tried walking along one of the branches before its legs were strong enough to support it?

I have a sense of what this verse is saying: for a bird, especially a baby bird, security and safety are found at home. When such a bird strays from its home, danger awaits. That danger could be a predator, a dangerously high limb, or its own careless curiosity. That part of the verse I understand. What does the rest of the verse mean by saying that "a man who strays from his home" is like a bird that strays from its nest?

Home means more than a house. We all grow up (or should) and leave our house. In a sense we leave home too—we leave Mom, Dad and younger brothers and sisters to go make our way in the big world. But in another sense we take home with us when we leave.

We take our identity with us. There are some things we never outgrow nor should we. Identity is one of those things. I am the son of Warren and Elaine Baldwin of Henderson, Tennessee. No matter how far geographically

I may be removed from them, I will forever owe my life and my sense of who I am to them.

We take our past with us. Connected with our sense of our identity are all of the memories, both good and bad, that shaped our lives when we lived at home. These memories form the mental and emotional grid that filters the world for us. From these memories we form opinions about people, about problems in life, about whom we will marry. Like it or not, these memories and this grid are with us for good. If we can accept these memories and learn from them, we can use them for our benefit.

We take our sense of the future with us. Actually we shape our future with the perspectives and values we learned in our home. The home life we experienced growing up gives us our identity. It gives us the memories that shape the way we view the world, and with this identity and grid, our homes give us our future. We will grow up, leave the house, take our identity and memories with us, and go build a future that in many ways will mirror the home from which we came.

That scares some people, but it doesn't need to. Remember, stray too far from your home, and you become like a little bird falling from its nest. The home from which you sprang is still your security base.

Was your home a healthy and secure place? If so, good, because then you will feel comfortable with this security base. Are you uncomfortable with the thought your home will always be with you because it was not ideal? Well, here is some good news—this is where we are different from a bird. We can change. We can study our lives, look at our grids, and say, "I want to change this picture. I want to create memories for my children that are happier and more positive than what I experienced. I want a brighter future. I want to include Jesus Christ while raising my children."

Even though you can't change where you come from, you can change where you are going. That is what Jesus Christ is all about. "Like a bird that strays from its nest is a man who strays from his home." God gives us families because they provide the shape and contours of our lives. Even with all of its faults and flaws, be thankful for that family! It is one of God's great blessings for your life.

ENSNARED

An evil man is snared by his own sin, but a righteous one can sing and be glad.

—Proverbs 29:6

My brother Bob and I were on a farm near Bozeman, Montana, when I heard something rustling in the tall grass. It was an animal. It wasn't running away but was struggling in one place. Slowly I edged in closer. The critter continued putting up a tremendous struggle to get away. I couldn't blame it!

Someone had set a small trap for varmints. But the trap didn't catch a fox or any other wild animal; it caught a house cat. Someone's pet had wandered from home, caught a whiff of some deliciously rotting meat in this trap, and set its sights, or its nose, in the direction of the alluring aroma.

Reality crushed whatever hopes this house cat had for dinner. When it stepped toward the meat and reached down to bite it, the cat triggered the mechanism and snap! the jaws of the trap came down upon the unsuspecting kitty, trapping its head and one leg in the contraption. It didn't snap hard enough to kill the cat, but it had the strength to hold the animal securely. The cat was tugging, pulling, and pushing, doing everything it could to get away, and even heightened its activity when I came walking up.

Carefully I stepped in closer, reaching in to release the lever. The cat tried to attack me, hissing, showing its teeth, and trying to claw me with its free legs. I was there to be the cat's rescuer, but in its pain and desperation, the cat presumed I meant to do it harm. I was there to help but was judged to be the enemy. Ensnarement does that. Desperation does that. It interferes when we try to discern who our friends really are or decipher good from bad behavior.

There is another proverb about ensnarement: "The evil deeds of a wicked man ensnare him; the cords of his sin hold him fast" (Prov. 5:22). This proverb is about the enslavement of a moral sin. It is about a husband or wife who refuses to be content at home, and they step out on their spouse. A moment of bliss or an evening of romantic pleasure may have all the allure and promise of rotting meat to a house cat on the prowl, but in time the pleasure will deliver reality: the snap of the trap. "The cords of his sin will hold him fast."

Sexual sins are not the only snares that await the unsuspecting. (See Proverbs 22:5.) Every time I see a teenager lighting a cigarette I think, "Oh, right now I know that seems so cool. But twenty years and $10,000 later, you will do almost anything to extricate yourself from this trap you have snapped onto your neck. You are trapped!" When I see college students pulling credit cards out of their wallets and saying, "Charge it," I cringe for them. In ten years their card payments may be running them $1,000 a month, enough money to purchase a nice car and house. They are ensnared in a trap they have snapped onto their own necks.

The first part of the verse reads, "An evil man is snared by his own sin." It is his own choices, his own decisions that have gotten him stuck. But he doesn't have to stay stuck. He might not be able to release the lever on the trap himself, but there is someone who can: God. It may take some heavy-duty repenting and changing of ways, but God promises relief. A man can surrender himself to God and become righteous. That is the promise of the second half of this verse: "But a righteous one can sing and be glad." A man who is free, or who has been freed, from a moral trap, a bad habit, or financial enslavement is able to enjoy the freedom from oppressive sinful or destructive behaviors. He is free.

Remember the cat in the trap? I found a stick, reached down with it, and released the lever. The cat was freed and ran for home. That is what ensnared animals and people want to do. That is what we need to do: head for home. That is what God promises.

THE WORD

Every word of God is flawless; he is a shield to those who take refuge in him.

—Proverbs 30:5

As a preacher I use the Bible as a tool for my sermons, Bible classes, and counseling. It is not entirely wrong to think of the Bible as a tool, but I often need to be reminded that the Bible is God's tool. Even when I am using it for a lesson or to provide instruction, the Bible continues to be God's tool to work in and transform the lives of people.

How do preachers and teachers use the Bible? We research the language and customs of the Bible, we study it, question it, and dig into its background. All of these approaches are entirely appropriate in the study of the Bible. We are, after all, trying to see and hear what the Bible has to reveal to us from God. So we preachers spend time over the Word, analyzing it, questioning it, applying it. We hover over it like a mechanic over an engine or a potter over clay, deeply involved and yet at times somewhat detached from it. We want to find the nugget that will preach. We make the Bible our tool.

Preachers need to be reminded that in the depth of our study, there is also a time for us to spend under the Word and its judgment on us, a time when we are not the mechanic but the engine. We are not the tool or the handler of the tool, but we are the engine itself that needs further repair.

The handler of the Word still needs to be handled by the Word, and that transition requires a change in thinking.

How do we approach scripture in a way that allows the Word to work on us? Rather than an approach that will result in a sermon or a Bible class outline, we need to approach the Word with an attitude honoring God as the potter and rendering us the clay.

Steve Gallagher, in At the Altar of Sexual Idolatry, provides four attitudes toward the scriptures for men who are mired in sexual addiction. The minds of these men are full of vivid, tainted pictures of human sexuality. These unholy mental images drive them to pursue unholy behavior. What can be done to change their mental imagery and eventually change their behavior? One very, very important thing the men can do is study the Bible and let the Bible work on and in them. They are the engine, and God through his Word is the mechanic. Steve uses James 1:21–25 to draw the four approaches or attitudes in our study of scripture.

One, have an attitude of repentance. "The unrepentant person who spends time in scripture only grows more calloused in his heart" (p. 250).

Two, be humble. "Many who spend time reading the Bible are doing just the opposite (of being humble). Rather than allowing the Word to penetrate and search their hearts and to bring conviction, they use it only to fortify doctrinal opinions or show others how much they know" (p. 250).

Three, have a devoted interest. "Look intently." How? You might do a verse-by-verse study using commentaries and different versions, meditate over every word in a verse, or memorize sections of the Bible. "To become transformed by the renewing of your mind (Rom. 12:2) means getting God's Word on the inside to saturate our lives" (p. 253).

Four, abide in the Word. That is, do what it says. "A person really only 'knows' the Word to the degree that he is living it" (p. 256).

We have the assurance that "every word of God is flawless; and he is a shield." But we have to penitently, humbly, and devotedly apply ourselves to that word and abide in it. Rather than submitting the Word to our techniques of study, we submit our lives to the operation of the Spirit through the Word (Hebrews 4:12–13).

RESPONSIBILITY

THREE WISHES

Honor the Lord with your wealth, with the firstfruits of all your crops; then your barns will be filled to overflowing, and your vats will brim over with new wine.

—Proverbs 3:9–10

My son Wes was six years old when we traveled to Jackson, Wyoming. That day we saw one elk, three moose, five deer, one badger, and two grizzly bear cubs. I was lost in the beauty of this wildlife menagerie when Wesley asked me, "Dad, if I could have three wishes, know what they'd be?"

This question was unprovoked. Even a little boy sitting in silence can wrestle with heavy thoughts. My son was. "Wes, I have no idea what your three wishes would be, but I'd love to know," I replied.

"I wish that my tooth would fall out. I wish that I never get any more stitches. And I wish that I never get sick again."

Simple. Nothing complicated. Three wishes totally free of materialistic selfishness or excess. His three wishes made a beautiful testament to the heart of a child.

So many of our wishes, those of us who are adults, are consumed with things, with money, with position. Our wishes are so far removed from the innocence and purity of a child who says, "I wish I wouldn't hurt anymore."

Can we adults simplify our wishes? Every year I continue to be astounded by the salaries some top athletes demand. I am amazed that some will hold out on signing their contracts because it is a million or two lower than some other guy. "I'm a better player so I should be paid more than him" is a frequent refrain.

Not all adults get caught up in the desire for money, possessions, and position. There are some adults who have purified their wish list. I remember seeing a Croatian woman interviewed on television during the war there some years ago. She stated her wish list, and it was a simple one: "We want food." I remember seeing a woman interviewed right after the LA riots. She said, "The stores have been robbed. How will we eat?" These woman have seen the downside of life. Their desires have been simplified. They are not asking for a new house, a new car, or a new TV. "We need food to feed ourselves and our children" is their simple prayer.

What are our needs? What do we really need? Sure, we need food and clothing, and Jesus assures us that if we faithfully follow him, he will provide for these needs (Prov. 3:9–10; Matt. 6:31). We need stable families (Deut. 6:6–25). God has been for that ever since he made family. We need love and acceptance, something we find in a stable home and a caring church (Rom. 14:1–2). We need salvation. We need to be saved from our own selfish drives and demands that complicate our lives here and crowd out meaningful life in the future (Matt. 13:22).

The purified heart of an adult becomes childlike. "Dad, if I could have three wishes, know what they'd be?" If we adults looked, we would notice that God has already met those needs.

PERSONAL RESPONSIBILITY

Guard your heart, for it is the wellspring of life.
—Proverbs 4:23

I have a friend who tells people, "Take responsibility. If you want to live a good life, you have to take responsibility for your decisions and your choices."

He usually says this to young people facing decisions about career and college. He says it to people facing the consequences of addiction and are wanting to blame someone else for their problems. "You can't blame anybody else. Maybe your parents did treat you badly; maybe you did have burdens dumped into your life that weren't your fault. But you are the one who made the decision to drink or pop pills. Now don't lay the fault of this problem at the feet of anyone else. Look at yourself in the mirror and say, 'I did this to myself.' Face it. Admit your problem and your guilt. Find others who can help you. Lean on God and pray."

At the heart of his message is the idea the Sage shares: "Guard your heart, for it is the wellspring of life." God blesses us with a pure heart at birth. When we become Christians, God again blesses us with a new start and a pure heart. But it is hard to keep the contamination of the world out for long. Before long negative thoughts, impure motives, and unholy lusts start to occupy our minds. God will purify us, and God will help us to walk cleanly; but we have to guard our hearts and discipline our minds. We have to take responsibility for the choices we make that affect our lives.

Steve Gallagher emphasizes this point in his book Break Free From the Lusts of This World (Dry Ridge, KY: Pure Life Ministries, 2004). Steve tells the story of James, a young pornography addict. James did not interact well with other children when he was young. He withdrew from kids his own age. As a late teen, he turned to pornography. He began counseling when he was in his twenties and went to twelve-step groups. Nothing seemed to help. In desperation his parents sent James to a Christian treatment center where he was given antidepressants. Five weeks later James attempted suicide. Another treatment center was tried, but James did not improve. He regressed emotionally, at times curling up into a ball and holding a teddy bear. James's withdrawal from people and the world was rendering him an infant again!

Finally his parents sent James to Pure Life Ministries, a Christian-based treatment center that emphasizes Christ's cleansing of our lives but also stresses the importance of taking personal responsibility for our decisions. Here James was encouraged to move from seeing himself as a victim, where his problems were everybody else's fault, to seeing himself as responsible for decisions he made that were harmful to his life, like viewing pornography. Eventually James became a new person. "Jesus Christ had come into his dark inner world and completely transformed him."

When James saw himself as a victim, he felt hopeless. But "when he saw that the problem was of his own making and that he needed to repent, immediately he saw also the way out . . . Instead of being furnished with excuses for his behavior, he was required to take responsibility for his actions. He was pointed to Jesus Christ who is the only answer to the problems we have created for ourselves, even if others contributed to those problems" (*Break Free*, pp. 117-18).

We can't control what other people have dumped into our lives, but we can give up a victim mentality and cease blaming others. We can "guard our heart, for it is the wellspring of life." We can take responsibility for our actions and seek the healing that Christ offers. We can experience that healing, with God's presence in our hearts.

PORN ADDICTION

Stolen water is sweet; food eaten in secret is delicious!
—Proverbs 9:17

The title of an online article promoting moral purity reads, "How To Raise Your Son to be a Porn Addict." Intriguing title, isn't it? It did what it was supposed to do—it lured me into reading it. The article by Steve Gallagher is subtitled "Tongue in Cheek."

Steve lists the following behaviors that will lead your son to an addiction to pornography: One, give him everything he wants because the more you do, the more he will become accustomed to having everything his way. Two, show him by your own example that pleasure is the most important thing in life. You don't have to be involved with pornography; indulging yourself in any pleasure will do. Help him see that he owes it to himself to indulge the desires of the flesh. Three, teach him to immerse himself in the mentality of this fallen world by watching television, reading secular magazines, and cruising the Internet. Four, teach your son that church attendance is something that is done out of obligation, not because one receives anything of value there. (You can read the whole article at www.purelifeministries. org/index.htm.)

Steve is not trying to lead people into porn addiction. He is showing how an addiction to porn develops. He has been there and knows the pitfalls, frustrations, and even death that awaits the unsuspecting who take the detour marked Pleasure. Steve is now dedicating his life to freeing men from the pursuit of finding meaning and fulfillment through unholy sensual pleasure.

I'll explain that last phrase: to free men from the pursuit of finding meaning and fulfillment through unholy sensual pleasure. God made us to be able to experience and enjoy sensual pleasure. Sensual pleasure is "of the body." We have several bodily or physical appetites that we seek to have fulfilled—hunger, sleep, and sex. God has provided the means for all of these appetites to be filled in appropriate ways: hunger in our stomachs is filled when we feed it with God's natural food; the need for sleep is fulfilled when with a good conscience we lay our heads down at night; and the appetite for sexual fulfillment is met when we keep ourselves chaste, marry a godly person, and devote ourselves to him or her for life.

But life gets complicated. With all three of these physical drives we can get off course and wreck. We substitute processed food for God's nutritious food, we substitute late-night TV watching and heavy doses of caffeine for adequate sleep, and we substitute all kinds of unhealthy sensual activities, such as pornography and promiscuity, for God's plan for marital sex.

We substitute cheaper alternatives for the godly means for satisfaction because we somehow feel the alternatives offer more pleasure or satisfaction. "Stolen water is sweet; food eaten in secret is delicious." But the drink, the food, the other person, or the erotic pictures are sweet for only a short time. They cannot meet the needs of our life. We cannot allow them to function as our meaning and fulfillment.

That is Steve's concern in addressing the issue of pornography. There is an attraction to it, or Americans wouldn't spend billions of dollars a year on it. But it is a deadly attraction. It is a stolen substitute for God's plan for fulfillment, so it can never do anything more than tease the viewer, finally frustrating him and even leading him towards dangerous paths, both physically and spiritually (Prov. 5:23).

As Christians, it is important that we learn that God is our ultimate fulfillment and that the needs of the body are met through obedience to his will. In the realm of moral behavior, that means dedicating ourselves to one person in life—our spouse—and avoiding all forms of stolen alternatives or substitutes, such as another person or even a picture of one.

LAZY HANDS

Lazy hands make a man poor, but diligent hands bring wealth.
—Proverbs 10:4

"You fellas move any slower and you are going to be doing yesterday's work." Ernest Borgnine said that to his ranch hands in the 1956 movie Jubal. Ernest played Shep Horgan, an affable ranch owner who loved his land and his men. But even the easygoing Shep couldn't refrain from a friendly reprimand of his hands when they shuffled about one morning.

John Wayne's inducement to his hands to work in the The Cowboys was "Let's go. We're burning daylight." This became a theme his young cowboys repeated later in the movie.

The old Westerns are a favorite movie genre for many people. One of the most endearing qualities of these classics is the old-time values they portray: values of integrity, family, pride, honor, and hard work as exemplified by the hero and heroine. Contrast this with the sloppy morals and loose character of some of today's movie heroes, and you can understand why the old Western classics are still popular fifty years after their release.

In their movies Ernest Borgnine and John Wayne tried to instill an ethic that God honored thousands of years ago: work. "Lazy hands make a man poor, but diligent hands bring wealth."

Proverbs are always true but may have a different application in different situations. As a general rule lazy hands do make a man poor, and diligent hands produce wealth. But don't we know people who worked hard all their lives and retired with very little? Several things can hamper financial success, such as bad timing, natural disasters, and economic downturns. In such cases diligent hands may not produce wealth, and that is no one's fault. Furthermore, in today's society, someone with a good idea can market it and get rich with comparatively very little work. They may have lazy hands but strike a gold mine the person with diligent hands never seems to find. It is a general rule though, that those who retire with something set aside had to work hard and save for that nest egg. Those who work as little as they can retire with as little as they earned. "Laziness brings on deep sleep, and the shiftless man goes hungry" (Prov. 19:15).

God instructs us on the honor and integrity of hard work. "The Lord your God will make you most prosperous in all the work of your hands . . . the Lord will again delight in you and make you prosperous . . . if you obey the Lord your God" (Deut. 30:9–10). God promised blessing to the people if they honored him and worked with their hands.

But this promise of blessing came with a warning: we must remember that all of our blessings, whether received as an inheritance for which we did nothing or received through our own labor, are ultimately gifts from the heavenly Father: "It is he who gives you the ability to produce wealth" (Deut. 8:18).

Work is out of fashion with a lot of people. When I was in college, it was hard to find replacements for my job when I would go away for a weekend. I couldn't find too many guys who wanted to earn some spending money by vacuuming carpets and cleaning bathrooms. It wasn't glorious, but it was honorable.

God honors what is honorable. He honors men and women who will work hard to support their families. Hard work reflects well on one's character. Refusal to work reflects poorly on one's quality of life and brings criticism from the Lord: "If a man will not work, he shall not eat . . . such people we command and urge in the Lord Jesus Christ to settle down and earn the bread they eat" (2 Thess. 3:10– 12).

So get busy so you won't have to do yesterday's work! Make good use of the daylight! Put diligent hands to the plow and overflow with thanks to God for blessing you with the ability to work. Use your blessings to his glory.

NOURISHING WORDS

"The lips of the righteous nourish many, but fools die for lack of judgment."

Proverbs 10:21

The word for "nourish" is "to shepherd." This is a farming term used in reference to shepherds who would lead their sheep from field to field in search of rich, nutritious grass. The work of the shepherd was to nourish his flock, making sure they had access to healthy food and water to keep their bodies healthy. Performed well, the shepherd's role meant that the sheep were healthy and robust.

Righteous people do the same thing with their speech. They are careful that the words they speak are "helpful for building others up according to their needs, that it may benefit those who listen" (Eph. 4:29). Righteous people know that words build, educate and encourage the lives of others, or they tear down, hurt and discourage. Since a righteous person is concerned about the health of his relationship with God and others, he consciously chooses to say only things that are constructive, helpful, pure and beneficial.

It is hard to do that. It is hard to so monitor our speech that we say only things that are constructive and godly and function for the spiritual and emotional benefit of other people. To practice this kind of communication, we have to practice an enormous amount of self discipline and restraint. Think of some of the normal speech patterns that we have to give up in the interest of being godly.

First of all, any kind of humor than denigrates another person on the basis of race, language, color, nationality or religious views is inappropriate. Humor that treats another person as less than human may really be a veiled attempt on the part of the speaker to appear superior to the one being denigrated.

Secondly, any use of humor that belittles or humiliates another person so the speaker can appear superior or smarter is not godly. Even if this humor is not motivated by the differences mentioned above, if it denigrates someone else, it is not nourishing so it does not promote godliness. Some people simply engage in hurtful humor against *anyone*, even family members and close friends, because they feel a sense of glee when they see another squirm or show embarrassment. This is often the humor of the mocker.

Thirdly, any humor or talk that is lewd or violates the moral sensitivities of other people is not constructive. "Obscenity, foolish talk or coarse joking . . . are out of place" (Eph. 5:4) for the righteous person who would shepherd others with his nutritious speech. Crude humor may be funny from a worldly perspective, but does it elevate the world's view of sexuality and morality, or does it keep it in the gutter? Does the joke or comment shepherd other Christians to keep their thoughts pure and to view sexuality from a family and godly perspective? If not, the joke or speech does not fall under the "nutritious" heading and should be avoided.

This view of nutritious speech may seem a bit rigid. But if you have ever been stung by inappropriate humor or verbal jabs from other people, you know how painful speech can be. There is nothing nutritious about jokes or comments meant to hurt and scar. So, the writer of Proverbs encourages Christians to avoid them. "The lips of the righteous nourish many, but fools die for lack of judgment." Fools die from lack of judgment because they don't exercise the discipline necessary to guard their minds and control their mouths. They give full vent to inappropriate humor and lewd talk. Ultimately, they have nothing of substance to offer anyone, not even themselves.

God wants our words to offer substance and blessing to other people. We can do that if we protect our minds from filth and make sure that the only words we allow to cross our lips are words that will build up, nourish, and improve the life of another. By our words we shepherd others into a deeper relationship with Christ and robust spiritual health.

INTEGRITY

"The integrity of the upright guides them, but the unfaithful are
destroyed by their duplicity."

—Proverbs 11:3

Integrity is the internal commitment to do the right thing under any
circumstance. People of integrity will be honest, decent and fair even if they
don't seem to personally benefit by their goodness. Indeed, being a person
of integrity might even cost you money. Consider a great American hero,
the automaker Henry Ford.

Many people remember Ford because of his creative bent with automobiles,
his genius in manufacturing (being able to mass produce his product with
speed and quality), and his fairness to his employees. I remember Henry Ford
because of his integrity, particularly as it relates to his respect for the young
men of America representing their country during war.

In 1917 and 18 the United States was in a brutal war with Germany.
It was an extremely expensive enterprise, costing America some 52 billion
dollars according to one American General who fought in the war, Smedley
Butler. In his book, War is a Racket, General Butler itemizes how much
profit some companies made on the war. From 1910 to 1914 Du Pont
made $6,000,000 a year. During the war years, from 1914 to 1918, it made
$58,000,000 a year. That is ten times as much as during peacetime. Central
Leather Company averaged $1,167,000 a year before the war. During war
time, in 1916, the leather company returned a profit of $15,500,000.

Remember, these astounding wartime profits were made during 1914
to 1918. During those years my great grandfather, a construction worker,
made ten cents an hour. That works out to 80 cents a day or $4.00 a week.
He would work two hours a day overtime, giving him an extra ten hours, or
$1.00 extra per week. On five dollars a week my great grandfather married,
bought a house and raised three kids. Great grandpa was making $5.00 a
week during the time the Du Ponts were making $1,000,000 a week. That
is incredible.

Henry Ford and the Ford Motor Company also made extra money during
WW1 but, Ford didn't like it. The industrialist said, "I don't want any of
it (the profits off the war). It's like taking blood money." Henry Ford felt
discomfort in making money off the shattered bodies of America's boys.

What was Ford supposed to do? According to the book, Populism vs.
Plutocracy, Henry Ford made the startling decision to return his wartime

profits to the government. He announced, "You can tell anybody and everybody that I am going to return it all."

Ford returned his wartime profits to the government, a total of $29,000,000. I'll repeat that. Ford didn't want to keep money he had made on the death and suffering caused by the war, so he returned to the government the money he had made during the conflict: $29,000,000.

"The integrity of the upright guides them . . ." People who act out of integrity do not look for recognition or reward. They do the right thing because it is the right thing. Having integrity actually cost Ford $29,000,000. Has he received any recognition for that? A government thank you note, maybe? How many of us are even aware of this story? The greatness of Henry Ford has yet to be told, and that greatness has nothing to do with automobiles. It has everything to do with integrity.

Proverbs 29:10 says, "Bloodthirsty men hate a man of integrity and seek to kill the upright." Ford is often criticized for his political and social views. I wonder if the basis for the criticism has less to do with the merit of his views and more to do with the envy of lesser men who hate the integrity of Ford?

Sometime today you will have the opportunity to do the right thing, not for recognition or reward, but simply because it is the right thing. Your upright behavior might even cost you, but know that you will be in good company.

ESCAPE

The righteousness of the upright delivers them, but the unfaithful are trapped by evil desires.

—Proverbs 11:6

A news story a few years ago focused on a man walking his dog. The dog ran off and the man trailed after him. He cornered the pooch in a gravel pit. All he had to do was walk through a puddle straight toward the dog and make the capture.

The puddle turned out to be more than a simple wet spot. The standing water had softened the dirt underneath. When the man stepped into the puddle, he sank up to his waist. He struggled and struggled but only succeeded in securing himself more firmly in the mud. The man spent two-and-a-half days buried in the waist-deep mud before someone came to his rescue.

I don't think this proverb about being trapped by evil desires applies to a man who is simply out walking his dog. It was in genuine concern for his dog that the man tried to walk through the puddle and rescue his pet. But even in his sincerity and innocence, he found himself helplessly trapped.

If the path of even the innocent can sometimes lead to snares and traps, how much more may the path of wickedness lead us into bogs and sinkholes we are totally unprepared for? I'm thinking of a friend of mine who took a particular liking to cocaine. He was single and had a high-paying job so he could afford the expensive stuff, or so he reasoned. But his addiction interfered with his concentration on the job, and he was fired. Now he had a very expensive addiction but no money to fund it. He could either enter crime in order to pay for his next fix or enter a rehabilitation program. He chose the latter.

One of his assignments early in his treatment program was to go back through the years of his using cocaine and determine how much money his addiction had cost him. The total money figure would reflect how much he had actually spent on the drugs as well any costs associated with medical or legal expenses he may have incurred.

My friend took his assignment very seriously. He determined how much he used on average a month, multiplied that by twelve and then multiplied that again by the number of years he used. He added in the hidden costs of abusing drugs, such as medical and legal expenses, just like he was supposed to do. He got his total figure and then just sat there and looked at what he had written on his paper. It couldn't be. Surely that was too much money! So he went back and figured again, taking great pains to be as accurate as he could in his assessment. But the figure came out to be about the same again.

How much had he spent on his cocaine addiction? One million dollars. That is a one with six zeros after it. That is a lot of money!

We were visiting in a living room during the recovery process when he told me his story of addiction and recovery. He told me about the million dollars. "A million dollars!" I said. "Man, how do you feel now?"

"Great," he said. "Never better. All I have is my clothes and a truck, but I'm clean. I just got a part-time job making minimum wage. I'm richer now than I've ever been."

"The righteousness of the upright delivers them, but the unfaithful are trapped by evil desires." Evil desires trapped my friend and kept him mired in that mudhole for about ten years. But he escaped. Another proverb promises escape for those who will seek righteousness. Proverbs 12:13 says, "An evil man is trapped by his sinful talk, but a righteous man escapes trouble." My friend escaped the mudhole of drugs and extravagant spending by desire, discipline, and the pursuit of godliness.

LOST IN THE WOODS

The path of life leads upward for the wise to keep him from going down to the grave.

—Proverbs 15:24

We moved from a city to a farm when I was eight. Our Vermont farm bordered a state forest with thousands of acres of trees, home to bears, mountain lions, and an invitation to three young boys to go exploring. Dad knew he had to prepare us for the challenges of life in a forest.

One evening Dad said, "Let's go, boys, we are going on a hike." We walked just deep enough into the woods to experience the tug of branches against our clothing and to lose sight of the edge of the woods. Deep enough to not know where we were.

"Who knows the way back home?" It wasn't me who asked that question. If my brothers Jim or Bob had asked it, I would have said, "Dad does." But Dad was the one who asked "Who knows the way back home?" Doesn't Dad know the way home? Panic struck three young boys.

My heart raced at Dad's question. I looked around and saw nothing but trees. The forest was so thick that when I looked up the trees seemed to reach to the sky, and only a small opening way above my head allowed even a glimmer of light through. It did seem rather dark now. One of my brothers began to cry, "I want to go home." I did too, very badly. This fun little excursion was not so fun anymore.

"Dad, do you now the way home?"

"Of course I do, boys. Just stay calm. I know the way."

"Then why did you ask us, 'Do you know the way home?'"

"Because I want you to begin thinking about direction. When you go to a new place or when you walk in the woods, you have to think about direction. In what direction did I begin my walk? In what direction must I return? Pay attention to signs. Do you see an unusual tree? A rock? The side of a mountain across the valley? Pay attention to these signs—they become road maps for your way back home. And occasionally take a look over your shoulder. Remember where you came from. Yes, I know the way back home." He took us there.

Twelve boys one time asked their leader, "Where are you going?"

"Home."

"Where is home?"

"It is with my Father. I am going there to prepare a place for you. You'll be going there, too."

"Lord, we don't know where you are going, so how can we know the way?"

"Just follow me. I am the way and the truth and the life. No one comes to the Father except through me. Remember, boys, direction." (John 14:-6).

Life sometimes seems like a forest of problems, deadlines, pressures, concerns, and worries that crowds out the light. We can all feel lost sometimes. Like an eight-year-old boy, maybe all we can do is look up at the light that is allowed in through the tops of the trees. And if that is the only light we have, that is good, because that is where our direction comes from anyway.

"The path of life leads upward for the wise," because they follow the Lord's direction.

LABOR

The laborer's appetite works for him; his hunger drives him on.
—Proverbs 16:26

As kids living in the country we had two large gardens and numerous animals, including two milk cows. Almost everything we ate throughout the year we raised and harvested. During the winter months we heated our house with wood we cut. We always had plenty to do, even if it wasn't what we wanted to do!

Do you know the word for tending a garden, canning vegetables, feeding animals, milking cows, and cutting firewood? Chores.

Chores is a bad word for a lot of people. On a beautiful summer day when there are three long rows of beans and peas to weed, wood to split, and a barn to clean, a lot of other more enjoyable activities come to mind, like walking along the creek, building forts, and playing baseball.

Truth is, we had time for those other activities. Jim, Bob, Carol, and I worked, but we certainly were not deprived of fun time as well. We probably enjoyed splashing in the creek and hiking through the woods so much because we did have chores.

There is tremendous value in teaching children to work. For one, it is productive. Work is what has kept this world going since God first made man. Raising vegetables and animals, building houses, doing repairs . . . where would we all be if it were not for the hard work that so many before us have done? As we continue to work today, we are maintaining the civilization that our grandfathers and grandmothers have entrusted to us.

Secondly, I think work helps mature children faster. Put me in a group of teenagers and in a fairly short time I can tell you which kids have grown up doing farm chores or working in construction in contrast to the kids who have spent hour after hour in front of a television set. There is a difference in maturity, conversation, and seriousness between kids who have grown up working and those who have not.

Thirdly, getting up early and working hard teaches a child discipline. Some never learn discipline because they are never taught it when they are young. When they get older and have to work, they can't adjust. I have known nineteen-year-olds who have had six jobs within a year of graduating high school. Why so many? They couldn't or wouldn't work. They either quit or the boss "helped" them out the door.

Even though baseball or fishing sometimes seemed to call louder to me, I loved the farmwork and cutting firewood that our country life required. My own kids were not raised under the same circumstances, but Cheryl and I tried to see that they had responsibilities and work to occupy their time and to develop their character. Later, businessmen and women from church gave Wesley, Jenny, and Kristin jobs, helping Cheryl and me to pass on the legacy of work to them.

"The laborer's appetite works for him; his hunger drives him on." If parental training, discipline, and honor don't drive a young person to work, perhaps hunger will. Any labor that is honest and honorable is worthy work. The sooner a young person learns that, the better prepared he or she will be to face life.

FOOLISH BLAMING

A man's own folly ruins his life, yet his heart rages against the Lord.
—Proverbs 19:3

An employee is late for work and gets yelled at by the boss. He gets upset and yells at a coworker. The coworker goes home and yells at her child. Not having anyone else he can dump his poisoned emotions on, he kicks the cat. It is always someone else's fault.

A hallmark of folly is that the foolish person blames everyone else for his blockheaded decisions and irresponsible lifestyle. "It's not my fault. Maybe I did drink too much, but you should have quit serving me. Maybe I did drive drunk, but you should have taken the keys. Maybe I did speak disrespectfully to the officer, but you should have answered the questions." Not my fault. Proverbs is clear in this passage that it is the foolish man's "own folly [that] ruins his life," not anyone else's. What identifies a man's life as a foolish one?

The foolish man wants to go his own way. He thinks he knows what is best and right, at least for himself. "The way of a fool seems right to him, but a wise man listens to advice" (Prov. 12:15). His standard is the only standard; therefore, he has to be right, every time! "There is a way that seems right to a man, but in the end it leads to death" (Prov. 14:12). It doesn't matter how right you are if you are heading for a fatal crash, even if you are "wise in your own eyes" (Prov. 3:5).

The foolish man does not listen to advice. One reason the fool's way seems right to him is that he is not open to the input of others, especially people of wisdom. A man becomes wise by pursuing the wise insights of others and applying their counsel to life. "Listen to advice and accept instruction, and in the end you will be wise" (Prov. 19:20).

The foolish man lives without concern for the consequences of his behavior. He does not think about the impact of his behavior on other people, including family members. How the family of a fool suffers! The fool thinks only for the moment, motivated by thoughts of ease, pleasure, or selfish ambition. The fool does it his way, without regard for others.

The foolish man blames others. He feels safe casting blame. If he can blame others for his mistakes or sins, then he can be relieved of responsibility, guilt, and shame. There are no apologies for him to extend or repentance to offer before God, no amends to make to another person. He is free to go out and repeat his foolish behavior because the next time he gets burned, it will be someone else's fault again.

As the ultimate offense, the foolish man blames even God. "Why has God allowed this to happen to me? Why does God continually let me down?" are common accusations posed as questions against God as a cover for foolish behavior. How can God be held accountable for a lifetime of poor choices made by someone exercising a selfish and stubborn will?

It is the fool who ruins his own life. It is the fool who spends too much money and fails to save. It is the fool who fails to harness his passion and spreads it in the streets (Prov. 5:16, 20). It is the fool who talks too much and does too little. It is also the fool who, having made a mess of life, blames others, even God! "A man's own folly ruins his life, yet his heart rages against the Lord."

If a hallmark of folly is blaming others for our mistakes and sins, it is surely a hallmark of wisdom and righteousness that one assumes responsibility for his actions, whether good or bad. "Who can say, 'I have kept my heart pure; I am clean and without sin?'" (Prov. 20:9). None of us can. What any one of us can do is confess our sins and shortcomings and trust the grace and faithfulness of God to attribute righteousness to us. Rather than blaming God for their hardships, the righteous recognize in God the ultimate hope we have for our redemption.

THE POOR

He who is kind to the poor lends to the Lord, and he will reward him for what he has done.

—Proverbs 19:17

I had to read this verse a couple of times to catch it. God says, "If you are kind to the poor, I regard that as kindness to me. And I will reward you for the kindness you have shown."

Jesus said the poor are always with us. There will always be someone who needs help, someone who lost a job because of downsizing, outsourcing, a sagging economy, or illness. People in these circumstances need help. They especially need help around holiday time. Some stores put up a Christmas tree with the names and wish lists of local people who need gifts for their children. Prison ministries provide names to local churches to help supply Christmas for the children of inmates. Community food banks raise and distribute food for those who are financially stressed.

Proverbs says, "God regards any help you give these people as help you have given him." That should encourage a kind and generous heart!

But what about people who are poor because they choose to be? It is not because of downsizing, outsourcing, a sagging economy, corporate misdeeds, or illness that has them out of work. They just don't want to work. They may have discovered that social agencies and local churches are a great source of blessing even for those who don't want employment! What do we do with them?

In the New Testament the apostle Paul said, "If a man will not work, he shall not eat" (2 Thess. 3:10). Sounds harsh, but Paul has a purpose in offering this charge. He is concerned that men are idle. Because they had too much time on their hands, they became busybodies and caused trouble. One of the remedies is for them to "settle down and earn the bread they eat" (2 Thess. 3:12). That is, they should work.

I agree with that. But what about the children of those who refuse to work? They can't help it that mom or dad is an idler, a busybody or a lazy person. Should they go without food, too?

A verse like Proverbs 19:17 helps me process this problem. "He who is kind to the poor lends to the Lord." I can't always know the circumstances behind a person's poverty, whether it is due to factors beyond their control or if it is laziness. This much I can know: God sees and rewards the efforts of those who are kind to the poor.

This message is not limited to Proverbs alone. The prophets especially renounce those who neglect or abuse the poor. The Law and the Psalms extol the generous heart that shares with the poor. "Maintain the rights of the poor and oppressed. Rescue the weak and needy" (Ps. 82:3–4).

Even though I may never know the circumstances that create poverty for a family's life, whether it is beyond their control or is the direct result of their own choices, I can know that God is pleased with the person who is moved with compassion for the needy and steps in to help. "He who is kind to the poor lends to the Lord, and he will reward him for what he has done."

If you happen upon someone today who needs help, let your actions be shaped by the one who is concerned with the needy and is waiting to bless you for the good you choose to do.

REBUKE

Better is open rebuke than hidden love.

—Proverbs 27:5

Receiving rebuke makes me feel devalued. Giving rebuke fills me with fear and trepidation. Misunderstandings about rebuke generate negative thoughts about it. Rebuke is often thought of as criticizing someone, pointing out faults, and positioning them in to a corner. I've been on the receiving end of such an approach. That understanding of rebuke is false.

True rebuke is better than "hidden love." Hidden love is overlooking faults, destructive behavior, and spiritual danger someone might be in. Hidden love is fear. Hidden love is turning a blind eye to bad behavior and a deaf ear to offensive speech. Hidden love is not love. It is fear and cowardice.

Dan Allender and Tremper Longman III say, "Rebuke is bringing truth to bear in a person's life in the hope he will repent so the relationship can be restored" (Bold Love [Colorado Springs: NavPress, 1992], p. 181). Genuine rebuke is not cold criticism, faultfinding, or positioning someone in a corner. That perception of rebuke actually works against what true rebuke is supposed to accomplish.

If true rebuke is better than hidden love, then rebuke is open and honest love. True rebuke is loving a person enough to confront him about dangerous and unchristian behavior in his life. If you rebuke someone, it means you care enough about him to risk losing his friendship. Even if you rebuke someone in kindness, love, patience, and gentleness, you risk being rejected and hurt by him.

Rebuke is bringing truth to bear in a person's life because things are not right in his life. He needs to repent. He needs restoration with himself, with others, and with God. Rebuke intends to save a person's life and soul.

Rebuke can be very direct and forceful as when Peter told Simon to, "Repent of [your] wickedness and pray to the Lord. Perhaps he will forgive you for having such a thought in your heart. For I can see that you are full of bitterness and captive to sin" (Acts 8:22–23). Peter's approach is certainly open and honest! Simon was in great danger. He tried to buy the power of the Holy Spirit with money. Peter knew that degrading any part of the Godhead by reducing Him to material value was blasphemous and dangerous to one's soul. Hidden love would have kept quiet and allowed Simon to go on thinking he was fine, even though his soul was destined for death. Open and honest love demanded Peter to speak the truth for Simon's own good.

Rebuke can be indirect and subtle. A king took another man's wife and had her husband killed. The preacher wanted to rebuke the king but had to be careful for his own life. He also wanted to present the rebuke in a manner the king would receive. Therefore, he told the story of a rich man who stole a poor man's lamb and served it up as dinner. The king was furious and said the rich man ought to be killed! The preacher said, "Thou art the man." Nathan, the preacher, brought truth to bear to King David. Though indirect and subtle, this approach enabled the king to see his misdeeds.

In both stories the men rebuked saw their error and the tragic state of their hearts and repented. Both men were restored to God and experienced restoration in other relationships.

Is there someone in your life you see involved in destructive behavior: drinking too much, stifling the joy of others with a critical spirit, lying, and ignoring their own bad behavior? You hurt for them. You are concerned for their soul. For too long you have kept silent. You have practiced "hidden love." But hidden love really isn't love; it is fear. Better is open rebuke that is practiced with love and kindness. Real love risks the loss of another to bring truth to bear in their lives but carries with it the hope of repentance and restoration. True rebuke is possible because we trust in God's grace to grant forgiveness and restore relationships.

PRISON

A fool gives full vent to his anger, but a wise man keeps himself under control.

                                                        —Proverbs 29:11

Clanging bars, tight spaces, and rigid schedules . . . that is the stuff of prison. None of that fits my personality very well. On the occasions I have conducted Bible studies in prisons, the clanging doors were enough to keep me from wanting to ever live there permanently!

I visited an inmate in Lander, Wyoming. The guard took me to the library, a small converted cell with book shelves and a bench for prisoners to sit on, to wait for the prisoner to be brought out. With the shelves and furniture there was barely room to turn around. The guard told me to wait in the library and then he left. Fortunately, he did not close the cell door or I would have had an attack of some kind. Even with the door open, I felt confined. I stepped out of the cell and waited by the library, not in it. Prisons and jails are not for me. I can't handle the lack of any kind of freedom—freedom to move, travel, sleep in, stay up, select what I want for dinner, or go to my children's ball games. Prison life is not for me.

Yet, I am aware that there is more than one kind of prison. There is the kind of prison that has thick block walls, a concrete floor, and a metal door that makes an awful clanking noise when it closes. But this is not the only kind of prison people can find themselves in. There are many other prisons that are just as limiting, just as confining, and just as fearful.

One of those prisons is fear itself. It could be fear of people, fear of new things, fear of growth. If a child is not encouraged when he is young, if he is not nurtured by his parents, he can grow up fearful of almost everything and everyone. This fear makes it very tough for that person to venture out to new job opportunities or new relationships.

A thirty-eight-year-old man in recovery from alcohol addiction had to face his fear. He was a barroom brawler, tough as nails. But as he progressed in recovery, he had to deal with the negative emotions that drove him. He cried when he talked about his fear. I said to him, "You are a tough guy. A barroom brawler. But inside you are still a scared little boy, aren't you?" The man looked at me and with tears streaming down his face said, "I have been afraid of everything and everyone my whole life. That is why I drink—it helps me forget my fear. When I fight, everyone thinks I'm tough. But I'm really not." This poor man lived in a prison of fear.

Anger is another prison. Anger gone to seed becomes resentment with a lust for revenge. A person in this prison can become consumed with hunger to strike back, get even, or even get ahead in the battle against someone else. Little or no peace of mind can be enjoyed by the person with this angry bent. Even dinnertime with his family gets wasted as he thinks about how to strike the next blow at his opponent. If he successfully strikes that blow, he still can't relax because he has to defend against the retaliation that he knows is coming back his way.

Anger is a personal prison that could lead to a real prison, the kind with metal and concrete. "A fool gives full vent to his anger." If a man doesn't learn to reign in this negative emotion, the law will do it for him. He is already in a prison of anger. If he doesn't learn self-control, he could find himself in a prison of metal bars.

It is possible that prisoners locked behind bars may experience some freedoms that we on the outside don't: freedom from the negative, controlling emotions that erodes lives. No, I don't want to trade places with those guys in there, but I don't want to live under the false pretense of freedom out here when I may really be subjected to other internal prisons that are just as confining. Being consumed and driven by fear, anger, envy, greed, hatred, and self-pity is not freedom.

Jesus said, "You shall know the truth, and the truth shall set you free." Jesus frees us from prisons of negative emotions and the condemnation they can bring.

PRIDE

A man's pride brings him low, but a man of lowly spirit gains honor.
                                                          —Proverbs 29:23

It was a good movie set back in the "olden times," and I wish I could remember the name of it. It was about a young boy facing some of the problems of growing up. He was learning how to relate to girls, how to stand up to bullies, and how to work.

In one scene, the boy is trying to plow a field behind a team of oxen. Something goes wrong; the reigns get tangled or the animals don't move for him, but the boy gets extremely frustrated, throws the reigns down, marches to the edge of the field, and slumps to the ground in tears. His grandfather sits beside him. "Son, don't let it get to you. You're learning. You are going to meet a lot of rock walls that you don't know how to get over or around. You'll get frustrated. But don't let your pride get in the way. Pride brings a man down. It breaks him. You stay in there learning and struggling."

I saw that movie about thirty-five years ago, so I don't remember all the details. But I do remember two things about this movie. One, I remember its quality. It was in black and white and did not have a lot of fancy sound or visual affects. But it was a quality movie because it was more than just entertaining. It was educational. I remember my dad pointing his finger at the television and saying, "Now that's when they made movies that were worth watching!" Secondly, I remember that the grandfather was teaching the boy more than how to handle a team of animals and plow a field. He was teaching him about life: setbacks, struggles, failing, frustration, and pride. "Pride brings a man down." Maybe the movie director read Proverbs?

Other verses in Proverbs addresses the problems of pride, an exalted view of one's ability or value, and contrasts it with humility, a godly-based assessment of oneself. Consider these proverbs:

> When pride comes, then comes disgrace, but with humility comes wisdom. (Prov. 11:2)

> Pride goes before destruction, a haughty spirit before a fall. Better to be lowly in spirit and among the oppressed than to share plunder with the proud. (Prov. 16:18–19)

Before his downfall a man's heart is proud, but humility comes before honor. (Prov. 18:12)

What is it about pride that is so dangerous? Pride exalts the self. Pride places one above everybody else, whether in ability ("I'm better at basketball than you") or value ("I'm just better than you, period"). If this person is so sure of his or her ability and value, why do they need God? Or the Bible? There is a reason why "the Lord detests all the proud of heart" (Prov. 16:5), and that is because pride works against the "fear of the Lord" (Prov. 8:13).

Humility is the recognition of one's need for God. Sure, you may be a great basketball player and have great self-esteem. But where does your ability come from? To whom do you owe your very life? Who sent his son so that you could have more than just basketball skills? To the one who is humble and recognizes his need for God, God gives grace (Prov. 3:34).

Pride brings a man down because none of us are as good as we think we are. Ultimately our pride will prompt God to set us down to teach us that there is only one God, and it is not any of us. "A man of lowly spirit gains honor."

AN ANGRY MAN

An angry man stirs up dissension, and a hot-tempered one commits many sins.

—Proverbs 29:22

Ike Gravelle was an angry man. Angry. Ike was an accomplished cowhand, breaking horses on a ranch in Montana. He was regarded as hardworking and friendly by the other ranch hands. But some bug inside of him led Ike to steal a harness in Lewiston, Montana, in 1891, landing him in the state prison in Deer Lodge.

Upon his release Ike set up his own hog operation in Helena. He had a low overhead so he was able to sell his pork cheaper than any other hog farmer in the Helena area. The reason for his low overhead was discovered—Ike was rustling cows from area ranchers, butchering them, and rendering the whole animals in large cooking vats for his pigs. This "discovery" cost Ike six more years in jail.

Ike was very angry now, angry that life had dealt him such low blows. He was only twenty-eight years old and serving his second stint in jail. How unfair! In his anger and self-pity he was susceptible to the manipulations of another prisoner, Harvey Whitten, who was serving eighty–nine years for the murder of a sheriff's deputy. Harvey schemed to extort $25,000 from the Northern Pacific Railroad Company and use the money to get a new trial. His scheme involved blowing up railroad property, including passenger trains. But Harvey, the mastermind, needed an accomplice to do the actual dirty work. Enter Ike Gravelle.

Harvey composed some extortion letters which Ike smuggled out upon his release. Ike mailed them and waited. When no money came, he struck. On August 2, 1903, Ike set off an explosion that damaged a railroad bridge over the Yellowstone River, three miles from Livingston, Montana. The train, carrying 225 passengers, narrowly avoided disaster. Then, on August 4, a train hit a sack of dynamite placed on the tracks west of Bozeman. The train was derailed.

For four months in the summer of 1903, Ike Gravelle terrorized passengers and employees of the Northern Pacific Railroad Company. But like all angry terrorists, Ike's reign of terror was brought to an end. On October 18, 1903, two guards walking the track surprised Ike. They shot at him and gave chase on horseback. The chase continued the next day when Ike was finally captured at his old hog ranch.

Ike received ten years for extortion. But when he went to trial again for theft of dynamite, Ike managed to secure a pistol made available by an accomplice. He used this to escape, and in the process, he killed a deputy and took his sidearm. What followed was pistol action reminiscent of the cowboy shoot-outs seen in the movies. When Ike saw he was not going to make his getaway, he turned his pistol on himself. Thus ended the first Unabomber rampage (Salina David, "Ike Gravelle: Montana's First Unabomber," Speaking Ill of the Dead: Jerks in Montana History, Dave Walter, ed. [Guilford, CT: Globe Pequot Press, 2000], pp. 99–115).

"An angry man stirs up dissension, and a hot-tempered one commits many sins." Ike was an angry man. When he sinned, instead of simply suffering the consequences of his bad decisions and paying the price, he fed his anger and kept plodding along in his sin and rebellion. "For as churning the milk produces butter, and as twisting the nose produces blood, so stirring up anger produces strife" (Prov. 30:33). Ike was churning inside! Even with the rebukes he received from the law, rebukes in the form of prison sentences, Ike would not change. "A man who remains stiff-necked after many rebukes will suddenly be destroyed—without remedy" (Prov. 29:1).

Anger and insensitivity to warning and punishment have killed many men and destroyed innumerable relationships, along with goodwill, friendship, marriage, and family. Give your anger a rest. Repent. Confess. Forgive. Do it today. The life and relationship you save may be your own.

WISDOM IN RELATIONSHIPS

PREACHERS VS. WIDOWS

To fear the Lord is to hate evil; I hate pride and arrogance, evil
behavior and perverse speech.

—Proverbs 8:13

One of the teaching styles of Jesus was to contrast conflicting outlooks
or practices. One such dramatic contrast is found in the Gospel of Luke.
Jesus said, "Beware of the teachers of the law. They like to walk around in
flowing robes and love to be greeted in the marketplaces and have the most
important seats in the synagogues and the places of honor at banquets. They
devour widows' houses and for a show make lengthy prayers. Such men will
be punished most severely" (Luke 20:45–47).

I can imagine some of these teachers of the law strutting around
in their self-importance. They are experts in the law and are skilled in
communicating it. Their expertise puts them in demand; people come to
them for interpretation and advice. Their expertise earns them recognition
and position so, they get the important seats at the religious and community
functions. Their enhanced position gives them advantage over those in
lesser positions, such as the widows. They also make a show of piety by
their lengthy prayers.

I can picture these religious leaders living like this because I have seen
religious leaders. Success in any field breeds confidence, confidence breeds
overconfidence, and the next step is arrogance. I've seen successful preachers
in demand for lectureships and meetings not have time to answer questions

from or give needed advice to younger preachers. I've seen preachers turn down meetings where they were offered a handsome remuneration because even that "was not enough for what I am worth." I've seen preachers who wouldn't tolerate even slight disagreement with their views. (I want to make clear that this categorizes only some preachers I know, certainly not all or even most of them).

I don't know if this modern parallel is exactly like that of the Jewish leaders in Luke 20, but to me it is too close for comfort, especially when Jesus says, "Such men will be punished most severely." Jesus surely didn't like this approach to life and ministry because, besides his stern warning against it, he offers a contrast.

"Jesus saw the rich putting their gifts into the temple treasury. He also saw a poor widow put in two very small copper coins. 'I tell you the truth,' he said, 'this poor widow has put in more than all the others. All these people gave of their wealth; but she out of her poverty put in all she had'" (Luke 21:1–4).

Among the disenfranchised of the ancient world were the widows. Unless a husband left her well-off or she remarried, a widow had a very tough time financially and legally. Jobs were tough to come by, and she often didn't get a fair shake in court. The Old Testament warns numerous times that men should not take advantage of the lowly position of the widow. The reason the men had to be warned of that is because they often took advantage of the widows. The religious leaders in Jesus' story "devoured" (took over in some way) the houses of these poor ladies.

This widow in chapter 21 attracted Jesus' attention. She did not let her lowly economic or legal state deprive her of an exalted spiritual one. She had God in her heart. She loved the Lord. She wanted to serve. She was willing to give anything and everything that she had, and she did. Two little coins, lepta, the smallest coins in Palestine at the time. It was all the woman had and she gave it all.

The rich gave out of their abundance. This woman gave out of her poverty. The rich, the ones in position to deprive this woman, were dismissed by Jesus. The woman was exalted.

I know religious leaders, and I know widows. I know who often have the letters, the credentials, the training, the confidence, and the position. And I know who gets praised by Jesus. I'm not knocking training and learning . . . but to those of us who are religious leaders . . . let's watch our hearts. We can never let training and position take the place of a heart devoted to service to God.

PRAY AND TALK

The tongue of the wise brings healing.
—Proverbs 12:18

A seminary student got into an argument with one of his professors about how to interpret a particular verse in Philippians. Understandably the student was worried the rest of the day. An unforgiving teacher can be a real threat to a student's well-being!

The student prayed about the situation. As he continued to pray and reflect upon his classroom experience, the student realized more was at stake here than a disagreement over a passage or even his fear of his teacher. The student feared male authority figures. He wondered, "Where did this fear come from?"

The student reflected upon the only real male role model he had in his life: his father. He recalled his dad's belittling treatment of him. His father never listened to anything he said. Communication between them was futile, even painful.

Summoning strength through further prayer, the student went home to visit his father. "Dad, may I speak with you?" he asked.

The conversation was very much one-sided. Dad was reading a newspaper when the conversation started and never put his paper down. The son poured out his heart: his anger toward his dad, his penitent spirit, his desire for a healed relationship.

Dad's response was at least a little condescending: "That's all right, son," Dad said. "That's how every kid feels about his dad." That was the end of the conversation.

Feeling less than positive about the experience, the son went on with life. But at a later time his mother asked him about the conversation. "He's been acting differently ever since then," she said, such as spending more time with a younger son who was still in the home. Then the mom explained to her son how the dad had harbored hard feelings toward his own father and had never resolved them before his death. These hard feelings against the leading male role model of the family had become multi-generational. It took prayer, honesty, and open conversation, but this vicious cycle was broken. In time the father and son established a good relationship with each other (Craig S. Keener, Gift Giver: the Holy Spirit for Today, [Grand Rapids: Baker Academic, 2001], pp. 126–27).

"The tongue of the wise brings healing." The first part of this verse says, "Reckless words pierce like a sword." Harsh words have a cutting effect in our hearts and lives. Sometimes the painful words are spoken thoughtlessly, but they can still cut and maim. At other times painful words are spoken intentionally. Some people intend to carve a plug out of your heart with a bit of gossip or ridicule. The lasting effect of such verbal violence can be long-term mental stress, spiritual lethargy, intense anger (even hatred), and multi-generational disruption. Cutting words can turn people who should be friends into enemies and sabotage close family relationships.

But "the tongue of the wise brings healing." There is always hope for such disrupted relationships if at least one person in the family or group can humble himself to seek God's will, study his Word, and pray. Pray for strength, for purity of heart, for the working of the Holy Spirit, and for healing in the relationship. Then talk. Talk kindly and gently with a view toward resolution. No, there are no guarantees but, there is hope as long as we trust God's power to bring reconciliation into our lives.

AN ENCOURAGING WORD

An anxious heart weighs a man down, but a kind word cheers him up.

—Proverbs 12:25

Anxiety is a form of fear, fear of failure, fear of not having done well enough, fear of not being good enough.

Christians often experience anxiety over their salvation. "Have I done what God has commanded? Am I living in his grace? Has he forgiven all of my sins, even ones I have forgotten and haven't named to him? Am I saved? If I died today, would I lose my soul, or would I be in heaven?"

You can get a sense of the anxiety Christians experience by asking them if they are saved. Ask them if they would go to heaven if they died today. Usually the answer is something like, "I hope so." In that lack of certainty, anxiety is born. Fear has found a foothold.

Not all of our fears are as deep and theologically oriented as questions of salvation. Many of our anxious thoughts center around things, such as the ball game, our first date, and making enough money to pay the bills. These are all important issues but certainly not of the caliber concerning fears about our eternal destiny.

Whether our fear is about something relatively trite, like if we'll score a basket in the game, or extremely significant, like if we are going to heaven, our fears are very real to us and very important.

The Sage understood that. He understood that "an anxious heart weighs a man down." An anxious heart robs us of energy during the day, and it keeps us up at night. It disrupts our focus and disturbs our peace. An anxious heart is not pleasant.

Time and experience teach us that if we look at our worries in context and think far enough ahead, we can reason ourselves out of anxiety. Most of what we worry about won't come to pass.

But there is another source of comfort to us when we are anxious: the presence of an encouraging person. "An anxious heart weighs a man down, but a kind word cheers him up." Some people are blessed with insight into another's heart and concerns. They seem able to read the signs of someone's distress and they have the compassion to settle their anxiety. They speak words that lift spirits and enliven hearts. These people are encouragers. So important is their ministry that the Holy Spirit has actually gifted them with the ability to do their work for the benefit of others (Rom. 12:8).

Why don't we see more people with this gift? Why don't we exercise it more ourselves? Maybe our own hearts won't allow us. Charles Swindoll writes, "There are those who seem to be waiting for the first opportunity to confront. Suspicious by nature and negative in style, they are determined to find any flaw, failure, or subtle weakness in your life, and to point it out. There may be twenty things they could affirm; instead, they have one main goal, to make sure you never forget your weaknesses. Grace killers are big on the "shoulds" and "oughts" in their advice. Instead of praising, they pounce" (Grace Awakening [Nashville: Word, 1990], p.62).

There are those who look for the fault and the failure. But thank God for the gracious man or woman who, having received grace from God for their own shortcomings, are willing to dispense with some of that grace to their anxious friends and neighbors. They have found an important key to a peaceful heart: grace received and grace shared helps to dispel the fear from an anxious heart.

ANSWERING HARSHNESS WITH KINDNESS

A gentle answer turns away wrath, but a harsh word stirs up anger.
—Proverbs 15:1

Have you ever received a harsh word? Critical remarks, negative comments, gossip, sarcasm, and mockery are all forms of harsh speech. How do you respond when such speech is directed at you? Anger? Harsh words stem from anger within the person who uses them, so they tend to prompt anger in the person who receives their sting. You might offer harsh words in retaliation. But there is another response: kindness.

There are three reasons for responding to harshness and anger with kindness. One, kindness surprises harshness. Anger produces harshness in the angry person. The person's harsh speech then produces anger in the person to whom it is directed. Anger expects and anticipates more anger. So if someone is angry at the world, at their childhood upbringing, or at you, and they treat you harshly, they are dumping their venom on you. Do you know how they expect you to respond? In anger. So surprise them. Kindness disrupts the expectations of the angry person and disarms their attack. The angry person doesn't expect you to fight fire with cool water. Remember Proverbs 15:1, "A gentle answer turns away wrath."

Secondly, kindness trips up harshness. Anger breeds anger. Harsh words expect harsh words in return. "An angry man stirs up dissension" (Prov. 29:22). Anger expects anger. So when you respond in kindness, what can anger do? It is temporarily confused. The angry person doesn't know what to do. The angry person may become more angry. He may erupt in rage. However, the angry person may just back up, catch his breath, and calm down. "A gentle answer turns away wrath."

Thirdly, kindness shames harshness. Anger's effectiveness is in its ability to shock, shame, and hurt its victims. The purpose of the anger directed at you is to force you into retreat. The angry person wants to intimidate you to back down. Anger knows what to do when you react in anger to its harshness. It rears up, squints its eyes, gnashes its teeth, and explodes! "An angry man stirs up dissension, and a hot-tempered one commits many sins" (Prov. 29:22). When you respond in kindness, you confuse the angry man. You may even shame him.

When we treat an angry person with kindness, we are acting redemptively toward him. We are acting like Jesus. Ultimately, what we hope happens when we answer harshness with kindness is that we open the person up to repentance, reconciliation, and restoration, to himself, with us, and with God.

Showing kindness when being mistreated isn't easy. To a tension-filled church Paul wrote, "Work out your salvation in fear and trembling." What did Paul mean? It is tough to be kind in a world of fighting. Tensions are high. People are anxious. Anger hangs in the air. But the person following Christ's example is challenged to act redemptively in a fallen world, which means to work toward reconciliation and spiritual wholeness.

Only the peace of God can dispel the anger in the world and within our hearts. We are the ambassadors of that peace. How do we do it? How do we answer harshness with kindness? A spirit of love must permeate our hearts. Love will show itself in two ways: tenderness and strength. Even a Christian who is kind does not have to let the anger of the world tear his life apart. "A gentle answer turns away wrath, but a harsh word stirs up anger." (The idea for this essay came from Dan B. Allender and Tremper Longman III, Bold Love, pp. 214–219.)

THE TONGUE THAT BRINGS HEALING

The tongue that brings healing is a tree of life, but a deceitful tongue crushes the spirit.

—Proverbs 15:4

I have felt the abuse of language. I've felt the sting of criticism. I've felt my face burn with embarrassment, anger, or hurt. That feeling reflects in facial expressions and burns deep into the heart. Those moments linger for a long time.

I have been on the receiving end of a verbal assaults, and I have been on the giving end as well. I hate to admit it, but I have used words that hurt people.

"A deceitful tongue crushes the spirit" may be understood in two ways. It may be understood from the angle of the person being lied about, or it may be understood from the perspective of the person who is lying. The crushed spirit may be in the receiver or in the giver. Consider the following.

A deceitful use of the tongue could be lying, gossiping, or maligning other people. Such speech crushes their spirit. "Reckless words pierce like a sword" (Prov. 12:18). Lives are ruined from deceitful speech. "A lying tongue hates those it hurts, and a flattering mouth works ruin" (Prov. 26:28).

James says the destructive power of the tongue is like a small spark that starts a forest fire. How many friendships do you know that have ended because of a misuse of the tongue? James also speaks of the tongue as a poison that can corrupt the whole person (James 3:5–6).

But there is a second way to understand the phrase "A deceitful tongue crushes the spirit." It could mean that such speech flows from a crushed spirit. We can only give what we have. A person who feels hurt or damaged operates from that pain and relates to others in hurtful, damaging ways.

He does that with a deceitful tongue, with words that hurt and crush those around him. "A malicious man disguises himself with his lips, but in his heart he harbors deceit . . . His malice may be concealed by deception, but his wickedness will be exposed" (Prov. 26:24–26). In this man's hurt and hate, he conspires to create this same pain in others. He may try to conceal his true intentions by appearing innocent or dismissing his painful remarks with, "Oh, I was only kidding." But the Sage says, "Oh no, he knows what he is doing." Hurtful speech issues from a hurting heart and creates that same hurt in others. Hurt people hurt people.

In contrast to this destructive use of the tongue, an honest and caring man uses his tongue to speak words of truth and wisdom, words of comfort and encouragement. "An anxious heart weighs a man down, but a kind word cheers him up" (Prov. 25:11).

An honest man, in an act of caring for you, may tell you (as opposed to telling everyone else) a truth about yourself that is necessary to hear but painful to bear. In this act of truth telling he is demonstrating care for you and may bring healing. His motive is not to hurt you but to help.

James acknowledges positive uses of the tongue. While he says that the tongue may be used to curse others, the tongue can also be used for blessed purposes, such as praising the Father (James 3:9). The tongue has tremendous potential for cementing relationships and building community if it is used honestly, kindly, and considerately. The godly woman "speaks with wisdom, and faithful instruction is on her tongue" (Prov. 31:26). Does anyone have a heart for building relationships more than a loving mother? Her wise, caring speech emanating from a godly demeanor, brings blessings to her family.

The tongue can bring life, or it can crush a spirit. How it is used is up to us.

KINDNESS WINS RESPECT

A kindhearted woman gains respect, but ruthless men gain only wealth.

—Proverbs 11:16

It tickles me how Proverbs says, "Ruthless men gain only wealth." Isn't that what ruthless men want—money? Ruthless in business, ruthless in crime . . . these kinds of men are not working for respectability, honor, or a good name. They are working to get ahead in the realm of the material and temporal. Money is one of the key indicators of success in this realm.

The Sage acknowledges that wealth is attainable by those who are honest and hardworking (Prov. 10:4–5). But he is also aware that there are ruthless men who put the dollar before everything else. They, in fact, can become ruthless in their quest for it.

The Sage considers such a man as foolish, evil, and wicked, unconcerned about neither God nor the community. Coworkers, friends, even family get hurt by such a foolish, evil man. This man may have wealth, but that is all he has. "Ruthless men gain only wealth."

Contrast this foolish man with a kindhearted woman. She may or may not have money. But the material things of this temporary existence are not her primary concern. She is kind. She treats others with gentleness and care. She treats them with respect, and she receives respect in return. This woman honors her community relations, and she receives validation from the community for her kind heart.

Of course, kindness is not the sole domain of this woman. God is deeply concerned that we all practice thoughtfulness in our relations with one another.

> Be kind and compassionate to one another, forgiving each other. (Eph. 4:32)

> Make sure that nobody pays back wrong for wrong, but always try to be kind to each other and to everyone else. (1 Thess. 5:15)

> And the Lord's servant must not quarrel; instead, he must be kind to everyone. (2 Tim. 2:24)

> Husbands, in the same way be considerate as you live with your wives, and treat them with respect as the weaker partner and as heirs with you of the gracious gift of life, so that nothing will hinder your prayers. (1 Pet. 3:7)

All of us are to show consideration and honor to our spouses, parents, and everyone. None of us are exempt from God's call to pour kindness from our lives into the lives of other people. As we live within God's grace and mercy and as we reflect his nature, treating other people with dignity and honor is something that will flow naturally from our Christlike hearts.

H. B. London, Jr., relates an experience in his life where he received kindness and respect, and how it encouraged him greatly. He was speaking before a conference of well-known religious leaders. His wife, Beverley, could tell that he was nervous. After his talk Beverley slipped her arm through H. B.'s, looked at him, and said, "I was proud of you tonight."

H. B. wrote, "I can't tell you how much that meant to me. The one who mattered most had affirmed me" (February 2005 Focus On the Family). "A kindhearted woman gains respect." The kindhearted woman is loved by her husband, her children, her friends, her church members.

We all have room in our lives for those special people who treat us with honor and importance. Also, we can aspire to be one of those special people who offer kindness and gentleness to the lives of others. Such a person will find kindness and respect returning to them from the people they have positively touched.

FIRE STARTERS

A scoundrel plots evil, and his speech is like a scorching fire.
—Proverbs 16:27

Scott Robinson asserted that he wasn't drunk or high when he set fire to his own house in Harrison County, Kentucky, completely destroying it. He did, however, admit he had downed "four or five shots" of scotch and had used methamphetamine in the days before the fire.

A woman in Zuelpich, Germany, tried to kill some spiders in her garage. Hair spray didn't kill them, so she tried to burn them with a lighter, igniting the hair spray. The fire swept through her house. "It's now uninhabitable," a police spokesman said, adding the spiders were gone, too.

When three men in Waipukurau, New Zealand, put fuel in their car that they had stolen from a farm, the car wouldn't start. Police reported that they put diesel into their gasoline-engine car. They examined the fuel pipe, police spokesman Ross Gilbert said, with a lighter, which naturally set fire to the car. The vehicle was a total loss. The men were charged with theft but nothing else. "There is no criminal charge for stupidity," Gilbert said (Quotes from "This Is True," Louisville Courier-Journal, Reuters, Reuters, Fri. Sept. 23, 2005).

These are true stories about "fire starters." Even in their tragedy, they are somewhat funny as well. Torching your own house. Igniting hair spray to kill spiders. Examining a gas tank with a lighter. I suppose there is room for some sympathy for these people, too. But how much?

These stories share common features. All of the stories are about individuals who were fire starters. All of the stories have a touch of humor. The people caused tremendous damage to property and put their lives at risk. And none of them meant to start the fires. None of them. But the innocence of their intentions can not erase the fact of the fires.

I've seen a lot of fires. I don't mean the kind like in these stories, but the kind that burn in people's lives and burn in relationships. That happened to a friend in college. Some of his dorm mates gave him a nickname they thought was humorous. If they had kept it in the dorm, all may have been fine. But the name got out and spread across campus. Here was a serious guy, an upperclassman, trying to conduct himself with honor and dignity on a Christian campus, but he was laughed at every time his nickname was used. Whether they meant to or not, this guy's friends started a fire, and he transferred to another school. "A scoundrel plots evil, and his speech is like a scorching fire."

Another student, this time a girl. A rumor started about a dating relationship she was in. That's all it was, a rumor. But to those who heard it with relish, it was too interesting and intriguing to keep to themselves. It was the kind of story that just had to be retold. It was told over and over, without any thought to the truthfulness of the allegations or the affect it would have on the girl. Before the rumor could be disproved, the young lady felt too much embarrassment to stick around and she moved on. "A scoundrel plots evil, and his speech is like a scorching fire."

Fires. Some are started with matches, but some are ignited with words. "With his mouth the godless destroys his neighbor" (Prov. 11:9a). James said, "The tongue also is a fire, a world of evil among the parts of the body. It corrupts the whole person, sets the whole course of his life on fire, and is itself set on fire by hell" (James 3:6).

A fire set to a house, a car, or another person's reputation may not be intentional. But once the fire gets started, the intention doesn't matter. The fire will rage, and property and people can be destroyed. Great care must be given to matches . . . and to the use of the tongue.

Fortunately, matches and speech can be used in positive ways, for constructive purposes, when we use them under the influence of God's Spirit in our lives.

WATCH WHAT YOU SAY

Even a fool is thought wise if he keeps silent.
—Proverbs 17:28

People love to talk and express their opinions. It often doesn't matter whether other people want to hear those opinions or not!

Ecclesiastes 10:12–14 says, "Words from a wise man's mouth are gracious, but a fool is consumed by his own lips. At the beginning, his words are folly; at they end they are wicked madness—And the fool multiplies words." I don't know if I like that verse! That is a harsh truth for someone who earns his living by talking, like a preacher. It is also pretty harsh for people who don't chew on their words before using them. It is certainly harsh for people who think they know most of the answers. Proverbs and Ecclesiastes both counsel that often the best thing to say is nothing.

When are such times? One time is when you don't know what you are talking about. Deep inside we probably know when we are speaking from knowledge or when we are just making noise. Another time to be silent is when comforting someone in grief. If you know how they feel from your own experience, you have earned the right to speak. If you really don't know, silence is best. They will appreciate that you care and will appreciate that you aren't pretending to know how they feel.

It is often wise to say little when you are in educational settings. What if you are a teacher and someone asks you a tough question but, you don't know the answer? Sometimes it is best to just say, "I don't know." Otherwise, you may pretend to know more than you really do and will get caught.

It is wise to say nothing when tempted to give unsolicited advice. For some people, such as a preacher or teacher, giving advice is part of our job. The longer we are in these professions, the more people tend to ask us questions. There are two things I've learned about giving advice, though. One, people usually wait too long before they ask for help; and secondly, people don't want our advice unless they ask. If you need to give advice, remember Ecclesiastes 9:17, "The quiet words of the wise are more to be heeded than the shouts of a ruler of fools." Life is complicated, and advice is often cheap and wrong. Speak quietly. Speak less.

Speak less especially when it comes to talking about others. Consider the advice of Ecclesiastes 7:21–22, "Do not pay attention to every word people say, or you may hear your servant cursing you—for you yourself know in your heart that many times you yourself have cursed others." Have you ever overheard someone talking about you? How did it make you feel? How did you respond? Next time, let them off the hook— isn't that what you would want?

Say little in the presence of God. Who hears everything you say? God. Ecclesiastes 5:2 says, "Do not be quick with your mouth, do not be hasty in your heart to utter anything before God. God is in heaven and you are on earth, so let your words be few." Ecclesiastes 5:4–6 cautions the worshiper to "not let your mouth lead you into sin." Sometimes it is in our silence that we glorify God and sense his presence in our lives.

When have we said too much? When our speech harms others. We know we are crossing a line when the information we are giving is not for the good of others but is for our own attention. That is the time to remember that even a fool is thought wise if he keeps silent, and to reign in our tongue.

STRIFE AND HONOR

It is to a man's honor to avoid strife, but every fool is quick to quarrel.
—Proverbs 20:3

Men do a lot for honor. They work long hours, stretch a double into a triple, and score the winning basket. All of these quests for honor are admirable, but they are not the highest level of honor to which we can aspire.

An overlooked realm for honor is in the control of our emotions. We are easily provoked by the immature and rude. Their cutting remarks sting us and invite retaliation. No one blames us if we respond in kind, verbally castigating our antagonists and putting them in their place.

While such a response may seem justified, it is actually unnecessary. Proverbs says it is to a man's honor to control his emotions when they are being prodded by a verbal abuser. It is to a man's honor when he holds his tongue, calms his nerves, and offers kind words, then just walks away. To his honor this man avoids strife.

To honor means to show esteem, acknowledge value, and be respectful toward. Men strive in the public arena of sports and work to gain honor, but a neglected arena for honor is our own character development. To maintain a smile at an adversary stoking the fires of discord and dissension and to simply walk away without striking back is worthy of respect and esteem.

The fool has no such control over his emotions. He is quick to spout off. He looks for an opening to verbally spar with anyone; and if he can't find such an opening, he creates one. The fool lacks the character to restrain himself by holding his tongue.

"Terry" was barred by a community baseball board from coaching a youth sports team. The panel of men and women met to discuss Terry's public behavior on the ball field. "Terry gets mad a lot. When he does, he berates the kids. He screams, yells vulgar words, and even cusses the umpires. I propose we forbid him from ever coaching in this league again."

"I second the proposal," another board member said.

After the board's vote Terry was barred from coaching even his own children in the youth baseball program.

This is a true story. If this happened to you, wouldn't you feel devastated? Sadly, it didn't disturb Terry. Proverbs says he is a fool. When told by a sports board of directors that "you are too hotheaded and we don't want you coaching for us anymore," Terry did not say, "Oh, I'm sorry. I'll try to do better. Please give me another chance after I've proved my character has developed." Instead, he tried to argue in a vain attempt to prove that he doesn't argue!

Because he is a fool, the quarreler is unable to see his own faults. He can't see the irony of arguing to prove that he doesn't argue. He keeps pressing his case with hotheaded devotion to his own opinions. It is precisely his blindness to his own lack of character and sinful dispositions that make him a fool.

The fool has no honor. He does not possess dignity or self-respect. He is a man to avoid.

The man who exercises verbal restraint and refuses to engage the foolish quarreler has inner strength. His living environment is peaceful and inviting to others. He builds a community of healthy people who encourage each other's character development. People of character recognize the value in themselves and others and treat each other with mutual respect and esteem, building a family, friendship, or church that is free of strife and dissension.

DEEP WATERS

> The purposes of a man's heart are deep waters, but a man of understanding draws them out.
>
> —Proverbs 20:5

I have been swimming in ponds so deep you couldn't touch bottom. I wouldn't want to touch the bottom anyway. Ponds are usually dark. What is in those deep waters? A tree stump? A tangle of branches and roots? A venomous cottonmouth snake? In Florida alligators are a big concern, because they are meat eaters. To an alligator, arms and legs are supper. I like to be able to see deeply into the waters I am diving into because potential danger lurks beneath the surface. The deeper and darker the water, the more likely danger waits an unsuspecting diver. I get that same sensation of depth, darkness, and danger when I look into people's hearts.

I take the Sage's words as a warning. A man's heart is deep. The greeting he gives you at work, the $5 he hands a beggar, and his role as a Little League coach may all be superficial, Proverbs warns. So, watch out. What you hear a man say and what you see him do may only be the surface of the water. Underneath the surface, deep in the murky stew, deep in the pond water of his heart, may lurk the dangers of tree stumps, a tangle of branches, snakes, and alligators. All of them are dangerous to the unsuspecting neighbor or coworker.

Who really knows what lurks in a man's heart? Proverbs says the wise man knows: "The purposes of a man's heart are deep waters, but a man of understanding draws them out." A wise man is someone who contemplates right and wrong. He observes how people make decisions and how those decisions work out. The wise man contemplates God and his will for our lives. After years of study and observation, the wise man understands life. This insightful man peers into the heart and says, "Oh, yes, I see, dark and murky. This heart is in trouble."

That is how Proverbs describes the heart: deep, dark, mysterious, dangerous. But the mystery of the heart is not totally unknown. A man of understanding can plumb the depth of the heart and see what is there, and he can draw it out. The man of understanding can also offer remedy for what is amiss in the heart. This is especially true of one who is an expert in matters about the heart: Jesus. In Matthew 15:18–19, Jesus said, "The things that come out of the mouth come from the heart, and these make a man unclean. For out of the heart come evil thoughts, murder, adultery, sexual immorality, theft, false testimony, slander."

All of these sinful attitudes and behaviors come from the deep waters of a man's heart. On the surface he may be a preacher and she may be a schoolteacher. Their professions are honorable and attract a lot of ethical, high-character people. But under the surface of their behavior is a heart with deep water concealing attitudes that might appall us. Peer deeply enough inside, and you might find greed, envy, and unresolved anger.

I don't want to read the Sage's warning and then run out and view everyone with suspicion! However, I don't want to dismiss these words from the wise man, either. So how can his words serve us?

One, by keeping our eyes open in all of our relationships. We are not looking for flaws in our friends and family so we can dispense judgment. But we encounter many life situations that tear at our hearts, such as sharp barbs of ridicule and arrows of criticism. We get shunned, rejected, and ostracized. Why? Why do people go out of their way to hurt us? "The purposes of a man's heart are deep waters." Beneath the surface of people's hearts are motivations and drives that may be dangerous and sinful.

Two, the Sage's words can serve us by causing us to look into the waters of our own heart. What internal motives propel us to be friendly? Are we functioning consciously and purposely as ambassadors for Christ? Or are we trying to work angles for some selfish pursuit? Are our words of praise for another person genuine expressions of admiration, or are they cheap flattery? Is our leadership in church or community a function of a spiritual gift, or is it a craving for recognition and affirmation?

The man of understanding may draw out the purposes of a man's heart from a coworker or friend. But the truly wise man studies his own life, analyzes his motives, questions his ambitions, and seeks to understand the deep waters of his own heart, and repent if necessary.

CRACKING ROCKS

> He who pursues righteousness and love finds life, prosperity and honor.
>
> —Proverbs 21:21

The Wind River Canyon between Shoshoni and Thermopolis, Wyoming, is a winding, narrow canyon with sheer rock walls rising from the floor of the canyon straight up to the sky. Ice can remain on the road through much of the day in later spring because the sun has limited time to cast its rays upon it.

Signs along the road warn drivers of falling rock. Numerous times I have had to slow down or veer suddenly to avoid a rock that had broken from the cliffs and plummeted onto the road.

What causes the rocks to break off and fall? Rock is hard. It resists blows against it. If you have ever tried to break a hardened rock with blows of a sledgehammer, you know how difficult a task it is.

The process that breaks large chunks of stone from its position and sends them hurtling downward is slow and patient. Snow-melt or rainwater drips and flows into the tiniest, most minuscule crevices in the rock formations, perhaps only a few drops at a time. Cold weather causes the water to freeze, creating a slight expansion of the water. Now the crevice is larger, even if ever so slight. But it does allow a few more drops of water to find its way into the opening. Cold weather causes another freeze and another slight expansion.

The process may take years, but the water and ice are patient. Over years, even decades, the water and ice force an ever-wider gap to appear in the stone. Finally, when sufficient volumes of water can pour into the crack and freeze, the rock can resist no longer. Its attachment to its base is severed, and the rock crashes downward, threatening destruction below.

The Wind River Canyon is beautiful and delightful to behold, but a drive through it is also a reminder that we must be alert. Even as we admire the beauty of the rock formations in the canyon, forces are at work to cause destruction.

Ice does that, and not just the ice caused by the freezing of water. There is another kind of ice, the kind that results from the freezing of attitudes and dispositions. Think of a man who cannot rejoice in the success of a friend but is envious of him. Instead of offering goodwill and congratulations, he drips the icy chill of envy into the tiny crevices of the relationship. When the envy freezes, the relationship can be severed. Think about the anger that seeps into the bond of a husband or wife. Instead of offering affection and love to each other, each feels anger and hurt. Instead of enjoying shared memories of fun and friendship, the only emotion they can muster is icy cold resentment. Each memory is like continued freezing until over time, the ice is victorious and causes a break.

The rock in Wind River Canyon and relationships share two things in common. One, they are both created by God and are to be enjoyed for their beauty. Two, they are both threatened with the destructive force of ice.

Ice is a cold, impersonal force, whether frozen water or frozen attitudes, that works with deadly patience. The only thing more powerful than ice, the only thing that can save rocks or relationships, is warmth. For the rocks it is the warmth of the sun. For relationships it is the warmth of love: "He who pursues righteousness and love finds life, prosperity, and honor" (Prov. 21:21); "Love covers over a multitude of sins" (1 Pet. 4:8); and "Love your enemies" (Matt. 5:44). Not even ice can defeat the powerful energy of God's warmth in our lives.

GOSSIP

A gossip betrays a confidence; so avoid a man who talks too much.
—Proverbs 20:19

Preachers get teased about talking too much. We do talk a lot. Some of it is expected, like sermons and Bible classes. It would be unusual for a preacher to stand up on Sunday morning and say, "I'm sorry, but I have nothing to say this morning." It might be unusual, but then again it might also be appreciated!

But the idea in this proverb is not about talking too much; it is about talking irresponsibly. There is a difference between someone who talks incessantly, even though that can be terribly annoying and unnerving, and someone who talks irresponsibly. Talking irresponsibly is connected to the first part of the phrase about a gossip betraying a confidence. Someone who talks too much can betray a confidence, but it is not the amount of the talking taking place that is the problem in this verse. It is the intent and the irresponsibility of the talker that is in focus here: gossip.

Gossip is a killer. Several verses in Proverbs address the problem of gossiping:

A gossip betrays a confidence. (Prov. 11:13)

A perverse man stirs up dissension, and a gossip separates friends. (Prov. 16:28)

Without wood a fire goes out; without gossip a quarrel dies down. (Prov. 26:20)

There is not much good that can be said about gossip. Gossip is more than annoying and unnerving: it is destructive. In Romans 1, Paul lists gossip along with sexual sins and murder as evidence of God's wrath being revealed against us. In 2 Corinthians 12:20, Paul lists gossip as one of the sins that he fears will disrupt the church.

God's teachers (Solomon and Paul) were both concerned about building healthy communities. They wanted families and churches to live together in openness, honesty, and love. They wanted people to live together in mutual respect and concern for the other.

Gossip undermines all of these healthy, constructive attitudes. Gossip is the opposite of openness and honesty. Gossip is conducted in quiet and in secret, hidden from the view of others. Its message is whispered and cherished as "choice morsels" (Prov. 18:8).

Gossip is the opposite of love and respect: you cannot love and respect the person you are vilifying with malicious secrets. Nor do you really love the person to whom you are passing on the delectable morsels, since you are drawing them into sin with you. Friends don't do that to friends. "A gossip betrays a confidence; so avoid a man who talks irresponsibly."

Both Solomon and Paul prefer words that are constructive, words that encourage, promote healthy community relations, and build character in others. For example, in Proverbs 10:21, Solomon writes, "The lips of the righteous nourish many." The word for "nourish" in Hebrew is "to shepherd." So the words of the righteous man "provides the nutrition necessary for the development of godly character" (Bland, p. 116). "Do not let any unwholesome talk come out of your mouths, but only what is helpful for building others up according to their needs, that it may benefit those who listen" (Eph. 4:29).

A gossip talks irresponsibly and destructively. He shatters community, whether in a family, church, or other social setting. But a wise man talks encouragingly and constructively. He talks responsibly. A wise man nourishes the hearts and minds of others. He builds community in human relations. He benefits those who listen by providing nourishment for the development of their godly character. The gossip or the wise man . . . which one do you think is blessed by God?

A GOOD NAME

A good name is more desirable than great riches; to be esteemed is better than silver or gold.

—Proverbs 22:1

A challenge of the proverbs is that they are so practical and applicable to life. We can't deny the clarity of their insight. Consider Proverbs 21:2: "All a man's ways seem right to him, but the Lord weighs the heart." That is powerful insight pressure-packed into one sentence. "Hey, guys, be careful how you live. You might think what you are doing is right and good, but God knows your heart." A verse like that reminds me that I need to keep reviewing my life by the standards of the Bible.

So many of the proverbs are so easy to grasp and apply to life. The Proverbs say what we wish we could have said. They elicit an immediate, "Yeah, I understand that." But not all of them are so easily understood and applied. For me Proverbs 22:1 is one such verse: "A good name is more desirable than great riches."

Do you believe that statement? Would you trade all of your money for a name that would be respected and honored? Would you work for a good name rather than a paycheck? See what I mean? I think there is quite a bit of value in that paycheck! I wouldn't want to try to live without it.

A paycheck allows me to buy my vehicle, make payments on the house, take the family out to eat, and send my kids to college. Give me a good name but take the paycheck away, and in a day or two, I'll be knocking on your door begging for food and a place to stay. It wouldn't take too long for me to lose that good name!

How then is a good name better than a paycheck or great riches? One, a good name may be your ticket to having any kind of paycheck at all so that you can support your family. If we understand "good name" as referring to living righteously, then it means your name is synonymous with honesty, integrity, and ethics. That is the kind of man or woman an employer wants to hire.

Secondly, a good name contributes to community, whereas great riches may not. A good name earned from loving and serving your neighbors means you are involved in helping others. You are loved and appreciated. Your kind behavior and gentle service have earned you a place in the lives of other people. That is community. No amount of money can pay your way into a loving community. You have to have a good name for that.

Finally, a good name outlasts earthly wealth and possessions. The bearer of the good name, the holy and saved name, the righteous name, will hear those great words, "Come, you who are blessed by my Father; take your inheritance, the kingdom prepared for you since the creation of the world" (Matt. 25:34). Great wealth will fade away; a good name will last forever.

I agree with Proverbs 22:1. A good name is more desirable than great riches. But this proverb, like many of the others, takes some time and effort to crack open and experience. It is worth the effort. Hopefully, the effort will challenge us not just with our understanding but with a commitment to obey. Sometime today we will be challenged with the ethical dilemma of being honest and maintaining our integrity or of denying that integrity and working for some selfish benefit. Don't capitulate. Don't do anything today that will compromise your integrity and with it, your good name, because a good name is more desirable than great riches; and it is certain to be blessed with God's approval.

SEIZING A DOG'S EARS

Like one who seizes a dog by the ears is a passer-by who meddles in a quarrel not his own.

—Proverbs 26:17

When I was twelve my family visited friends who had a German shepherd they had chained up. He didn't like his chains. While all eight of us kids ran, yelled, and played for hours, he kept barking and straining at his chain.

I loved dogs, so the shepherd on the chain won my sympathy. All day long he struggled against the end of his chain, barking, as if pleading for attention. I would give him some.

I approached the dog. As I came within reach of his chain, he jumped up and put his front paws on my outstretched forearms. Boy, he is happy to see me, I thought. Then, that mangy, ungrateful beast grabbed my left forearm in his mouth, bore down, and began twisting his head.

He wasn't playing. He meant to tear my arm off. If it wasn't for the heavy winter coat and thick shirt I was wearing, he might have seriously injured me. As it was, he bit through my clothing and into my arm. I didn't grab this dog by the ears. In fact, I tried to be a friend to him. But he wasn't my dog; and even though he was lonely and craving attention, he wasn't going to accept it from a kid who didn't belong in that house. "Like one who seizes a dog by the ears is a passerby who meddles in a quarrel not his own."

Angry German shepherds are not fun. Nor are quarrels. Tempers flare in quarrels. Facts become irrelevant as emotions take center stage. Good intentions, like my trying to pet the dog, are read in the worst possible light, and people bite back in some perceived need for self-defense. Quarrels are dangerous ground. Trust is wounded, kind feelings are betrayed, and friendships are lost. Avoid quarrels, both your own and the quarrels of others.

That holds true for some of the quarrels that go on at your work place. If something is not directly your business, don't try to make it so. Your good intentions (if that is what they genuinely are) will not be appreciated. Someone will take offense, and in time, some "German shepherd" will take a plug out of your arm. Or your heart.

That also holds true for your own family. Granted, there is a time for a mom or dad to step in and say, "Okay kids, knock it off!" Parents have to maintain peace in the home and teach the kids to love each other. At times that requires refereeing the quarreling bouts of the kids and even calling the match. But there also comes a time when parents need to proceed with extreme caution into the relationships of their children. Eventually those kids will marry. In their marriages they will experience quarrels with their spouses. A certain amount of that is to be expected. Maturing couples will weather those spats, learn from them, and move on. But sometimes a concerned, well-intentioned parent will attempt to intervene. "Like one who seizes a dog by the ears is a passerby who meddles in a quarrel not his own." It's a tough call, but parents must also continue to mature, and one manifestation of that maturity is that they let their married children process their own heated moments.

It is not safe to grab a strange dog by his ears. Sometimes it's not even safe to pet him! It is almost always equally dangerous to make someone else's quarrel your own. If you do, you are sure to get chewed on. Quarrels aren't pretty, but neither are the scars earned from unwise intervention.

READING HEARTS

As water reflects a face, so a man's heart reflects the man.
—Proverbs 27:19

Samaria was off-limits to self-respecting Jews. The Jewish population there mixed its blood with Gentiles, rendering it unfit for the covenant people to spend time there. Most Jews traveling from Judea in the south of Israel to Galilee in the north took a lengthy detour around Samaria rather than soiling their feet in the dust of Samaria. But Jesus was different. He traveled into the heart of the country.

Jesus met a woman there steeped in her Samaritan heritage. She told Jesus, "You Jews say we should worship in Jerusalem, but our people worship on this mountain." She stood up to Jesus. She knew the Jewish disdain for the Samaritans, and she was willing to share some of her own with Jesus.

You might get angry reading this story in John 4. There may have been people with credentials to stand up to Jesus, but this woman didn't have them. First, her moral life was a shambles. Jesus pointed out to her that she had five husbands and the man she was living with now wouldn't even share his name with her. Secondly, her spiritual life was barren. She brazenly admitted that her worship was as adulterous as her personal relationships: "Our people worship on this mountain," she said.

I read ignorance and brashness in the Samaritan woman's demeanor and speech. I don't know if I would have continued the conversation with her. But Jesus is on a spiritual mission. What kind of candidate is this woman for becoming a disciple?

Jesus read something different in her brashness. He read honesty. Underneath the repeated rejection by men, the shallow spirituality, and the vanity of her nationalistic pride was a purity of spirit that even many of the religious leaders lacked. Preachers were often rebuffed by Jesus, challenged, even attacked. But not this woman. Jesus stuck in there with her, countering her objections and disclosing his own heart.

Jesus revealed something to this woman that he refused to reveal to the arguers and debaters of the law. Risking personal disclosure, Jesus told her, "I who speak to you am he" (the Messiah, John 4:26). Crowds pursued Jesus. Pharisees pestered him. The court interrogated him. Everyone wanted to know, "Jesus, who are you?" The woman never asked, but Jesus told her, "I am the Messiah." I wonder, "Why tell this woman?"

Paul said that God chooses to place the treasure of the gospel in clay pots (2 Cor. 4:7). People are those clay pots. We are the vessels that carry the message of salvation to lost and dying people. We take the message of hope to a homeless man, a pregnant teenager, a crippled vet. We embody and proclaim the message of forever to people who can't see past today.

But certainly, some vessels are more worthy of bearing that message than others. In Jesus' day and ours, there are people who are bright, moral, and decent. They surely qualify as the fine china that should bear the treasure. But Jesus picked the five-time divorced, spiritually confused woman at the well to disclose his nature and bear his message to the rest of her Samaritan village. Into this common clay pot Jesus poured himself.

"As water reflects a face, so a woman's heart reflects the woman." Jesus can read the hearts of people. He could read the heart of this woman; and behind the pride, ignorance, and degradation, he saw something redeeming: honesty. Jesus read this woman without judgment or condescension. He knew her story and still offered her the opportunity to bear the treasure of the Gospel. She did. Every person we meet, even a woman at a well, is a potential vessel for God to store his treasure.

MOCKERS

Mockers stir up a city, but wise men turn away anger.
—Proverbs 29:8

Mockers are tough to deal with. They have sharp tongues that cut to the quick. They seem to lack any tenderness for other people.

Mockers are quick-witted. They always have a snappy answer, and it usually is sharp and penetrating. If they direct their remarks against you, others will likely laugh, thinking the mocker is hilariously funny. But you will feel the sting. You'll know there is something besides the face value of the humor. There is a sharp point that pierces your heart and your pride with barbs that keep the arrowhead painfully buried in your memory.

Mockers appear strong. If you challenge their humor with humor of your own directed back at them, you will likely lose. Your joke won't go over as well, or they will turn it back around on you. They already have the energy and momentum going in their favor. They already have the group laughing with them at you. If you challenge the mocker, you are going against a stacked deck.

Mockers seems to be well-adjusted people who are popular and well-liked. They seem to always have people around them. Those people are usually laughing. Some people are actually envious of mockers.

Mockers are quick-witted, but they aren't really strong. They appear that way externally, but inwardly, they are a raging torrent, and that rage actually makes them weak. The hurtful sarcasm is simply a way to keep people at arm's length. They lack self-esteem. They are often the ones who are envious of the higher character of someone else. They feel alone in a crowd because even though it looks like they are accepted by other people, they haven't accepted themselves. So despite appearances, mockers are not well adjusted. They are "stirred up" inside—uncertain of themselves, angry and struggling with poor self-esteem. That is why, according to Solomon, they "stir up a city." They project their uneasiness and discomfort onto everyone else with a biting, sarcastic humor that leaves other people hurt.

In contrast to the mocker is the wise man. The wise man may not be as quick-witted as the mocker, but he doesn't have to be. He is not engaged in any put-downs of other people. He values their relationship too much to embarrass them in front of others. The wise man not only appears strong;

he is strong. His inner strength comes from an assurance of the value God has assigned to him. The wise man is well-adjusted. He may not be popular, but he is recognized because of his calmness, his sense of value, and his fair treatment of others.

The wise man may not gravitate toward the center of attention like the mocker, but he doesn't need to. His strength of character is read by people who recognize the value of character. The influence of the mocker is to disrupt, disturb, upset. "Drive out the mocker, and out goes strife; quarrels and insults are ended" (Prov. 22:10). Mockers use their insults to "stir up a city" or any group they find themselves in. But the influence of a wise man is to impart wisdom, build others up, and calm the disturbance of the mocker. Wise men "turn away anger"—the anger of the mocker plus the anger the mocker creates in others.

One of God's blessings to us is the wisdom He brings to us through wise people. The wise offer a calm, soothing stability in our topsy-turvy world. They are powerful with a strength that comes from God—knowing his Word and living in relationship with Him. They pass this strength onto the rest of us with their well-spoken words: "A man finds joy in giving an apt reply—and how good is a timely word!" (Prov. 15:23). By the speech we use, we can all choose to be the means by which God blesses others with his influence in our lives.

Spiritual Living

SEE JESUS

Trust in the Lord with all your heart.
—Proverbs 3:5

My daughter Jenny asked an intriguing question when she was five years old. "How come Jesus can see us but we can't see him?"

I can understand a question like this arising in a child's mind, can't you? We tell children that God sees them and loves them, that Jesus is always with them. Can you let your mind go back far enough in time to when you may have wondered, "How come Jesus can see us, but we can't see him?" Maybe more recently you have wondered, "How can we trust in the Lord with all of our heart if we can't see him?"

I don't think it is just children who wonder about why we can't see Jesus. I think adults do, too. We may not expect to see him with our eyes, but don't we all want to "see" Jesus with our minds? Aren't there times we want a deeper affirmation of where he is and what he is doing? Don't we want to know that he is really at work in our lives? I doubt that I am the only one who has prayed, "Lord, show me what you want for me to do!"

I can understand a child wanting to know why we can't see Jesus because I have wondered that myself sometimes. "How come Jesus can see us, but we can't see him?"

The answer is, "We can see him. No, maybe not him personally, like the disciples did when Jesus was here on the earth. But still there are ways we can see Jesus."

We can see him in worship, when the songs we sing speak to our hearts, when they lift us from sadness and despair and give us a sense of hope for the future. The songs and the Lord's Supper remind us that the trials and temptations we bear today will be short-lived, defeated by the victorious return of Christ. In that way we see Jesus.

We can see Jesus in the character of his people around us. Jesus ministered to people with physical handicaps, often healing them. We can't heal in the ways Jesus did, but we can minister in his name and in his character to those people. When you see someone assisting the blind or pushing the wheelchair of a man without legs, you are seeing the heart of Jesus at work in one of his servants.

We can see Jesus in the spirit and disposition of people who forgive, who rise above insult and gossip, who render love to those who are unloving. When Jesus prayed, "Father, forgive them because they don't know what they are doing," he raised the bar for all of us in the realm of reconciliation and relationship building. If Jesus could forgive even as the nails were holding him suspended, all to promote healing and reconciliation in relationships, there is not much we cannot forgive. When you see that forgiveness, you are seeing Jesus at work in a person's heart.

So, Jenny, we can see Jesus. He is manifest in the lives of his faithful servants. We see him in the disposition and behavior of those who call themselves "Christian." So go ahead, "Trust in the Lord with all your heart."

SEXUAL ETHICS FOR SINGLES

> Keep away from the immoral woman, from the smooth tongue
> of the wayward wife. Do not lust in your heart after her beauty
> or let her captivate you with her eyes.
> —Proverbs 6:24–25

Solomon deals with sensitive issues, moral purity being one of them. Here he is telling his son to be morally careful, instruction that works for sons and daughters.

We have a number of seemingly innocuous little phrases we use to justify our moral lapses. "It wasn't a sin. It couldn't have been. We really cared about each other." I've heard that sentiment numerous times from individuals trying to excuse themselves: a thirty-five-year-old preacher who cheated on his wife, a middle-aged woman who met a "nice" guy in a bar, and a fifteen-year-old girl about her most recent encounter.

We use our strong feelings to cover or medicate our sin and pain (the people above knew that they sinned in having sexual relations outside of marriage, and they were in a lot of personal pain), but it doesn't work. We can speak of our strong feelings, but all that does is betray what we know inside: we did wrong, and we hurt because of it. Sexual relations need to be confined to our marriage partner, our husband or wife.

Many reasons caution us to wait until we are married to be sexually active.

One, we won't know if it is true love until we give or receive a ring with the accompanying commitment.

Two, if we start giving in to temptation before we are married, how can we be sure either of us will be able to resist temptation after we are married?

Three, saying no actually enhances people's respect for us. Giving in to another's demands diminishes that respect.

Four, sexual promiscuity puts us at risk for pregnancy or disease.

The four reasons above for remaining pure are all true. I've seen hearts and lives broken in all the ways the reasons above said they could be. But none of them are the best reasons for remaining pure. The best reasons for a Christian to say no to outside sexual activity are biblical, spiritual, and Christ-centered.

Look at 1 Corinthians 6:12–20. Here Paul gives a number of reasons for a Christian to keep his body from sexual activity outside of marriage.

One, the body is to be lived for the Lord, not sexual immorality (v. 13).

Two, God will raise the body. So the implication is that the body should be used for God (v. 14).

Three, our bodies belong to God, so they should not be used for fornication (v. 15).

Four, when we unite our bodies with someone immoral, we become one with that person (v. 16). We are supposed to be one with the Lord (v. 17).

Five, sexual sins are committed against one's own person, body, and life (v. 18).

Six, our bodies are temples of the Holy Spirit and should be used only for holy purposes (v. 19).

Seven, we are not our own. God bought us at a great price (Jesus), so we belong to him (v. 19b–20).

This passage "challenges the contemporary view that sex is a mere biological function that has no deeper moral or spiritual meaning . . . Many people today view the urge for sex simply as an itch that must be scratched" (Gregory Linton in Christian Ethics, ed. by Larry Chouinard, et.al. [Parma Press, 2003], p. 391). But it is more. "The sex act is not merely a function of the body. It is an act of our whole selves as sexual beings . . . It carries meaning whenever it is practiced" (Stanley Grenz, Sexual Ethics [Louisville, KY: Westminster, 1990], p. 217).

The fact that children reach puberty earlier than years ago and that people are getting married at an older age than years ago means that young people are facing, on average, ten years of suppressing sexual desire before they marry. That is a long time. As Christian people and as the church, we need to encourage purity among young people, offer a vision of purity and eventual marriage to them, and assist them in their spiritual walk and discipline. God would not have taught purity unless he knew purity was possible. Our kids need to know that, and they need to know that we are there to help them however we can.

To our sons we say "Keep away from the immoral woman, from the smooth tongue of the wayward wife. Do not lust in your heart after her beauty or let her captivate you with her eyes. Keep that sexual intensity and excitement for the one to whom you say 'I do.'" To our daughters we say "Keep away from the immoral man, from the smooth talk of the slick player. Do not lust in your heart after his empty promises. Wait for a young man who will honor the Spirit of the Lord within you and will treat you with the dignity deserving a young woman who has dedicated herself to the Lord."

STINGY WITH YOUR HEART

The righteousness of the blameless makes a straight way for them,
but the wicked are brought down by their own wickedness.
—Proverbs 11:5

This verse posits a contrast between a righteous man and an unrighteous man. The righteous man finds a straight path—he is moral, honest, and decent. People like him, and they trust him because of his commendable character traits. The unrighteous man is wicked. He lacks the commendable character traits of the righteous man. He is immoral, dishonest, and he eschews decency. The unrighteous man will be brought down by his wickedness.

Solomon doesn't specify all the possible forms of wicked behavior here—lying, cheating, murder. However, throughout Proverbs, he makes the point that any form of wicked behavior may ensnare a man (Prov. 5:22), bring him down (11:5), destroy his hope (11:7), and cause him to perish amid shouts of joy from those he has abused (11:10).

Wicked behavior is a problem. But there is an even greater, underlying problem—the attitude of heart. You've probably heard the saying, "Behind every successful man is a good woman." And that is often true. But there is implied in Proverbs 11:5 another saying, "Behind every wicked behavior is an evil attitude or disposition." Proverbs 11:6 also addresses this idea. Solomon writes, "The righteousness of the upright delivers them, but the unfaithful are trapped by evil desires."

People recognize the blameless man. There is a depth of character that goes beneath observable surface behavior. You see a righteous man do a good deed. That is simple enough. But the truly righteous don't do good deeds to draw attention to themselves; their good behavior stems from a deep commitment to being good. That is character.

Just as a righteous man has a well from which pours out his good behavior, so the unrighteous man has a well from which pours forth his wicked behavior. When a wicked man lies to your face, smiling as he does it, and when he seduces a girl, berates his wife, and crimps the spirit of his children, he is drawing from a deep spring of depraved attitude and spirit. "For out of the overflow of his heart his mouth speaks" (Luke 6:45).

"He is trapped by his evil desires," Solomon says. When the wicked fall, people cheer (Prov. 11:10). They cheer because they are weary of the offensive behavior of the wicked.

Occasionally, even the wicked themselves grow weary of their offensive behavior. They may want to change. They may see the profitable relationships of the righteous and desire such relationships for themselves. But when they make any attempt to change their wicked behavior, they find the task of transitioning from unrighteousness to righteousness is not as easy as they might have supposed. They find that before they can actually change their behavior, they must first change the water in the well they have been drinking from. That is the hard part! The unrighteous are trapped by evil desires. The cords of their sin hold them fast (Prov. 5:22).

There is hope for the man who wants to change. Proverbs 4:20–27 counsels appropriate behavior for one who does not want to stumble and fall into sin. But it could also serve as counsel for those who want to leave unrighteousness. One statement in particular stands out: "Guard your heart, for it is the wellspring of life" (Prov. 4:23). Be stingy with what you let in; refuse to dwell upon unwholesome images; confess evil thoughts to a trusted mentor; pray for God's cleansing. Guard your heart and experience God's cleansing power in your life.

CRAFTINESS

A good man obtains favor from the Lord, but the Lord condemns a crafty man.

—Proverbs 12:2

The owner of a small company wanted to pass on the daily operations of his business to someone he could trust. He would handle the financial responsibilities but sales and distribution would be given to a dependable supervisor.

Most of his employees were contract workers. To determine which worker to promote to manager, the owner gave some of them new responsibilities that would test their skills and honesty. They would work unsupervised and be responsible for turning in their hours. The owner would base his judgment on who to promote on the basis of honesty in reporting time.

No one knew they were being tested. But one of them would have an opportunity to become, for all purposes, the owner of the company. That person just had to be honest.

One employee saw an opportunity here. Not an opportunity to prove herself both capable and honest and thus "inherit" a business, but an opportunity to make a few extra dollars on an unsupervised project. The woman either dragged the project out or padded the hours. Either way, she failed to prove her dependability and lost out on a major promotion. "The Lord condemns a crafty man." The boss "condemned" the crafty woman. In a small way, she was rewarded for her cunning—she made about one hundred extra dollars over a weekend job. But her craftiness cost her much more. Not only did she not become the manager of the company, she didn't receive any more contract work, either.

A crafty person is one who "keeps his thoughts secret. They are secret because he is making plans to hurt others" (Bland, p. 125). He is contrasted with the good man who pursues wisdom and the good of the community—traits that God honors. The crafty person employs scheming, cunning, and guile. Secrecy cloaks his motives and intent. The crafty person lacks character. He is not the good man whom the Lord favors (Prov. 12:2a). What are some traits of the crafty man?

The crafty man thinks only of himself. He does not think about the good of the group. The scheming of the crafty person pits him against everyone else for recognition and promotion. He is always conniving, looking to gain an edge over others. He may work within community to foster his own ends, but he does not work for the good of the group. His behavior does not build goodwill within the community.

The crafty man thinks only for the moment. He does not think long-term. A small victory today is better to the schemer than a major victory tomorrow that is based on hard work, honesty, and community spirit. The schemer would rather tweak the facts to make one hundred dollars in the short term than to be honest and own the business in the long run.

The crafty person thinks only of his own wants. He does not think, "What would God have me to do in this situation?" God's goals or perspectives really can't compete with the schemer's agenda. On the job, at home, or in church, the schemer does not employ a godly perspective or ethic. He can't seem to get past his own selfishness. "The schemes of folly are sin" (Prov. 24:9).

"A good man obtains favor from the Lord, but the Lord condemns a crafty man." A good man pursues the good of others, thus building a good life for himself and positive community spirit. A good man pursues God's will. He will practice honesty and integrity simply because God honors such attitudes. Ultimately a good man practices godly wisdom, and his behavior will eventually trump that of the foolish crafty man.

MEN WHO ARE TRUTHFUL

The Lord detests lying lips, but he delights in men who are truthful.
—Proverbs 12:22

The Lord in not the only one who detests lying lips. My dad does. The severest punishment my siblings and I received as kids was reserved for lying. I still remember him saying, "I hate a liar." I grew up thinking that the person who lies has a serious character flaw. Well, turns out he does. The Lord hates lying lips.

Marion is a friend of mine from Wyoming. For years he had his own construction company. "I can understand a man who would steal one of my tools from the job," he would say. "I didn't like it, but I could understand it. He may have wanted to use it on another job or sell it for some cash. It was wrong—it was stealing. But there is some rationale to it. But lying? That is lower than stealing. A thief can return the tool he stole or buy you a new one if he has a change of heart. But a liar . . . how can he return his deceitful, destructive words?"

Liars are thieves. They don't steal tools or stereos, but they steal nonetheless. They steal your goodwill. They steal your trust. They steal your innocence. They steal truth, the necessary sinew of all healthy and productive relationships. Remove that sinew, remove that truth and trust, and what is left to hold love, service, and devotion together? That is why whenever a sin like adultery is committed, lying is always present. Furthermore, what often hurts the offended spouse more than the actual adultery are the lies of the guilty partner: "Honey, I would never cheat on you! How could you even suspect me of that? You know I love you and am always faithful." When the lying and adultery are both uncovered later (as they almost always are), which one do you think hurts the deepest and longest? It is no wonder that the Lord hates lying lips. It is a wonder that we tolerate them so.

But a man or woman of truth is a person the Lord takes delight in. A person of truth is solid. He or she rests on principles of honor, character, and integrity.

People of truth can be counted on to do their job, to go straight home after work, to speak words that are honest. Their honesty may hurt at times. Their words may be piercing and penetrating, but their words can be trusted. Their words have the potential, if offered in love, of binding people together and building strong community. "Truthful lips endure forever, but a lying tongue lasts only a moment" (Prov. 12:19). Oh, the hurt and memory of the lying tongue may last for longer than a moment, but the person may not. Who wants to remain in the company of someone who lies to you? It is the person of honesty we welcome into our lives, the person of character and integrity. With them we can build relationships.

I think that is why the Lord delights in honest people. God wants people in relationship with himself and with other people. An honest person can contribute to that dynamic. A liar cannot. A liar tears apart the fabric of honesty and with it, the hope of love, friendship, and relationship. That is why the Lord hates lying.

FOUNTAIN OF LIFE

The fear of the Lord is a fountain of life, turning a man from the snares of death.

—Proverbs 14:27

A preacher was in his office one afternoon when the phone rang. He picked it up and said, "Hello." A man's voice on the other end asked, "Preacher, do you baptize at your church?" The preacher suspected either a prank call or a phone salesman. But he said politely, "Yes, in fact we do baptize." "Okay, well," the man continued, "do you have a problem with pond scum in your baptistry?" "Oh no," the preacher said, "we will baptize anybody."

He was a good preacher. I don't necessarily mean by the way he handled the phone call. I mean by the theology of his answer. "We will baptize anybody."

This story appears in a popular e-mail. Even though it is meant to be a joke, it prompts the question, "Who may be baptized?"

People often have a sense that they have to be a certain kind of person to be baptized. They have to have a certain level of Bible knowledge, go to church so many years, and be "good" before they are worthy. Those individuals think they have to have the Bible, church, God, and everything else figured out. If they have all these ducks in a row, then they are ready.

I am glad to say that anybody who thinks that is wrong. Anybody who thinks they need to have all these things figured out is putting too much pressure on themselves. Preachers and teachers of the Bible don't have all these things completely figured out! We are still studying and learning.

Baptism is for anybody at any point in his or her life who realize their need for God. They are ready when they realize the way they have been living is not the right way to live. When they believe Jesus Christ as the only one who has the complex answers to life and confess him as Lord of their life, they are ready to be baptized as an act of obedience to God's rule over their lives.

Baptism really is for anybody and everybody. Even, as the caller asked the preacher, pond scum? I don't like designating anybody by that kind of denigrating term. But I do need to tell you that anybody, no matter how badly they have lived their lives, can come to Christ for new life. That new life includes baptism. Romans 6:1–4 says that anyone who has been baptized has left their old life behind and is now living a new life.

In 1 Corinthians 6:9–11, Paul writes that the sexually immoral, the idolaters, adulterers, homosexuals, greedy, drunkards, slanderers, and cheaters would not inherit the kingdom of God. They would not see God, and they would not be with Jesus. However, Paul says that this does not have to be the final statement for their lives! They can leave those lifestyles, seek God, and be baptized, sanctified, and justified in the name of Jesus. Yes, baptism is for anybody. It is for anybody who realizes they are sinners, they are lost, and they need Jesus Christ.

I feel badly for people who get trapped in lifestyles that diminish their self-worth and leave them feeling used and broken. Drugs can do that. Crime. Sexual misbehavior. Disruptions in the family. Lying. These sins diminish us, makes us question our value, and can even make us despair of life. But I have a message for anyone who feels this way: those feelings do not have to be the final statement of your life. God promises you a new life in Jesus, and you can have it today, with God's fountain of life.

ENVY

A heart at peace gives life to the body, but envy rots the bones.
—Proverbs 14:30

The first part of this verse is calming and soothing. A heart or mind that is happy and contented, filled with good thoughts and intentions, rooted in God and home is a mind that is at peace. This man can lay his head comfortably on his pillow at night, knowing his priorities are in order, his emotions and behaviors under control, and his life healthy and happy. He is at peace.

Not so the envious man. The envious man is diseased, stricken with a condition that "rots" his bones. He is afflicted with attitudes that attack his spirit. His peace of mind is upset. His emotions are raging and his behavior malicious. His life is in disorder. He is corrupting and dying from within.

What is envy? Envy is the desire for what another person has. It may be the desire for another's good looks, car, bank account, position in life, or family. Envy is what we feel when we look at who we are and what we have, compare it with another person's, and become very dissatisfied with our lot. "Why can't I have his or her good looks? Why can't I drive a car like that? Why can't I have their money? Why can't my family be happy like their family is?

This comparison displays a lack of gratitude for how God has blessed us. A lack of gratitude makes us hungry for more. When we see that someone has more, we want what they have. That is envy. Envy left unchecked can develop into an angry and vicious disposition.

Envy starts out as an attitude but then works itself out in despicable, unholy behaviors. One girl threw acid in the face of a prettier girl. That is envy. A skater hired hit men to injure another skater and bump her from the Olympic team. That is envy. A teenager ran a key down the side of a classmate's new car. That is envy. Envy is even associated with the crime of arson. The arsonist reasons, "Why should you have a nicer house than I do?" He watches the hard work, possessions, and dreams of a family go up in smoke, and he smiles inside.

Envy can become so intense that it will be satisfied with nothing short of the death of the one envied. Why do you think Cain killed Abel? Envy not only says, "I want what you have!" it also says, "If I can't have what you have, I'll see to it that you don't have it either! I'll destroy what you have and who you are!" Hence the scarring of a pretty girl's face, the skater's damaged knee, the scratch on the car, the torched house, and the lifeless body of a brother.

Envy can be more subtle than these violent behaviors. Envy can manifest itself in violent speech. Think about what motivates gossip. Who benefits from it? It is not the one being gossiped about. The only one who can possibly benefit from gossip is the one doing the talking. The gossiper tries to undermine a coworker so he has a better chance for the promotion. Or he may simply want to tear down the reputation of the one being reviled. Gossip is a subtler form of killing the one we envy.

"There is no gratification for envy, nothing it can ever enjoy. Its appetite never ceases, yet its only satisfaction is endless self-torment" (Henry Fairlie, quoted in Successful Investing in an Age of Envy [Ft. Worth: Steadman Press, 1981], by Gary North, p. 6). You can see why "envy rots the bones."

Envy cannot be satisfied, but thankfully, envy does not have to be left untreated. If envy is a lack of gratitude, then envy can be countered with gratitude. One of our greatest weapons in the spiritual arsenal God has given us is the ability to say, "God thank you for everything you have blessed me with! Please keep me grateful!" That is an important step in overcoming envy.

SACRIFICE OR SERVICE?

The Lord detests the sacrifice of the wicked, but the prayer of the upright pleases him.

—Proverbs 15:8

How can the Lord detest sacrifices when he commanded them in the Old Testament? The first four chapters of Leviticus are about the burnt offering, grain offering, fellowship offering, and sin offering. Each of these "offerings" was a sacrifice, burned on an altar, that Israel offered God. Then, in chapters 5, 6, and

7 of Leviticus, Moses runs through the sacrifices again, explaining them in further detail. God is the one who commanded the sacrifices and then reemphasized them to make sure the people understood how serious they were.

Then God says in Proverbs, "The Lord detests the sacrifice of the wicked." God says, "There are some circumstances where I do not want or accept your sacrifices. Even though I have commanded them as a means of reconciliation between us, there can be no real reconciliation through sacrifice without the accompanying ethic of a penitent heart."

The tension between obeying the command to sacrifice and obeying the command to be ethical is played out in Jeremiah chapter 7. Jeremiah was a fiery chap, given to great boldness in his preaching. He had to be that way; Jeremiah preached in Israel at a time when church activity was running at full throttle, but sin was also. People would live throughout the week as if there were no God, pulling dirty deals in business and abusing other people, and then assembling on the day of worship as if there were no sin. This is the situation Jeremiah faced. How did he handle it? He stood at the gate of the temple and preached. Here is part of his sermon:

> Hear the word of the Lord, all you people of Judah who come through these gates to worship the Lord. This is what the Lord Almighty, the God of Israel, says: "Reform your ways and your actions, and I will let you live in this place . . . If you really change your ways and your actions and deal with each other justly, if you do not oppress the alien, the fatherless or the widow and do not shed innocent blood in this place, and if you do not follow other gods to your own harm, then I will let you live in this place . . . Will you steal and murder, commit adultery and perjury . . . and then come and stand in this house which bears my Name and say, 'We are safe'—safe to do all these detestable things? . . . I will thrust you from my presence!"

Wow! That is a sermon! The people come to worship God at the house of worship in Israel and the preacher says, "Oh no, you don't. You can't live like there is no God during the week and then come worship like there is no sin. I want to see changed hearts, reformed ways." The sermon continues:

> Go ahead, add your burnt offerings to your other sacrifices and eat the meat yourselves! For when I brought your forefathers out of Egypt and spoke to them, I did not just give them

commands about burnt offerings and sacrifices, but I gave them this command: Obey me, and I will be your God and you will be my people.

"To do what is right and just is more acceptable to the Lord than sacrifice" (Prov. 21:3). God wants our worship, sure. But he wants that worship to flow from a heart and life that is devoted to him. Other Old Testament preachers echo this message: "To obey is better than sacrifice (1 Sam. 15:22). "For I desire mercy, not sacrifice" (Hos. 6:6). "The sacrifices of God are a broken spirit" (Ps. 51:17). Say your prayer today, read your Bible, and worship on Sunday. But along the way, don't forget to treat others with kindness and dignity, keep your heart pure, and be honest. These behaviors reveal the heart of one devoted to God. This is the heart that is prepared for worship.

PATIENCE

A man's wisdom gives him patience; it is to his glory to overlook an offense.

—Proverbs 19:11

Seventy years. That is how long the Babylonians oppressed the Israelites. Seventy years. That is roughly how long the communists oppressed Christians in Russia and Eastern Europe.

Seventy years is a long time. It is a lifetime. Children born in the early years of the communist oppression were old people before it ended. An estimated sixty-six million Russians and Eastern Europeans were killed by the communist machine that ran over the lives of those poor people. Sixty-six million!

Entire families were wiped out. Nearly every family in some countries, such as Ukraine, could count a family member or close friend who was shot, starved, or worked to death in the gulags. What a brutal time!

How could a person survive such an experience! One Lithuanian minister who survived the ordeal gave this report: "We tended to take the long view. Seventy years is not that long in the mind-set of the church. We knew the Communists would fail. See? It only took God seventy years to bring down a well defended, deeply entrenched political system. That's not bad!" (William Willimon, Pastor: The Theology and Practice of Ordained Ministry [Nashville: Abingdon Press 2002], p. 262).

I think seventy years is a long time. That is because I am programmed to think in terms of human existence. Seventy years is a lifetime. But the Lithuanian minister was able to endure his persecution because he didn't limit his thinking to this lifetime. He thought beyond. He was thinking of eternity. God is in charge of all eternity, and seventy years is a mere blip on a screen. Sure, there is discomfort, suffering, and offense. But in the perspective of eternity, it is only a breath.

"A man's wisdom gives him patience; it is to his glory to overlook an offense."

Communism was an offense. Think of all the widows, all the orphans, all the nervous breakdowns, all the lives shattered by that brutal system. It lasted for seventy long years!

Ah, yes, the Lithuanian minister could say (I'm putting words in his mouth, now).

> It seems like a long time, doesn't it? But lift up your eyes, look ahead. Look far ahead into the future. Keep looking. The future just keeps going. Know why? Because God is there, and we will be there with him. Seventy years of suffering isn't so long when God is making the journey with you. So no matter what your suffering, hang in there, be patient. A godly patience will help you overlook and endure an awful lot of offense. If we Russian and European Christians could survive with patience the offense of communism, there's not much else the rest of you can't endure with a little bit of godly patience yourselves.

It is with some degree of shame that I think about some of the offenses I have suffered that I cling to and cherish. We think that being wronged by someone gives us an edge over them. We now have a basis to critically judge them, look down at them, and discredit them to others. The Lithuanian preacher says, "No, give it up. Put it behind you, go on. We did. You can." Proverbs says, "Give it up. Practice wisdom and godly patience. Overlook the offense. Forgive. Go on. That is to your glory."

PURE HEART

Who can say, "I have kept my heart pure; I am clean and without sin?"
—Proverbs 20:9

Man can do just about anything he wants to. Not too many years ago we watched the first man walk on the moon. I was ten years old. Imagine putting a man in a spaceship and sending it out into outer space. That was the stuff of mythology, but we saw it play out on our television sets. What can't man do?

Even years before we had advanced technology, man dreamed of reaching out into the universe. He dreamed of ascending into the heavens and seeing what was there. Man didn't have rocket fuel or a rocket, so he had to envision and develop other means of reaching beyond himself.

No problem. Man stacked one block on top of another and began his ascent into heaven. We have no idea how tall man's tower stood. We can only guess how far into the sky it reached. But we do know that man's attempt at reaching the heavens and developing a name for himself caught the eyes of God. God said, "If as one people speaking the same language they have begun to do this, then nothing they plan to do will be impossible for them" (Gen. 11:6). God wasn't pleased with this attempt because it demonstrated that man could do just about anything he set his mind to. So God halted the building project and scattered the builders. The name of the place was called Babel because God confused the language of the world (Gen. 11:9). Today, "babble" refers to any senseless or meaningless conversation.

Man can do just about anything. In ancient times we attempted to reach the heavens. In modern times we have. But man's accomplishments do not end there. We can communicate with someone on the other side of the world in a matter of seconds. We can take a damaged heart out of a person's chest and put a new one in. Severed limbs can be reattached. Is there anything we can't do?

Yes. One thing man can't do is keep his heart, mind, and life pure. "Who can say, 'I have kept my heart pure; I am clean and without sin?'" No one can say that. Man can do a lot, but in the end, much of what he does is babble. It is senseless, meaningless noise. The thing that is most important, keeping our standing with God, gets disrupted when we assert ourselves and try to prove how capable we are. We move away from God. We determine our own course and set our own values, and as a consequence we stain our heart and mind.

David, the great king of Israel, realized this. He prayed to God, "Create in me a pure heart, O God, and renew a steadfast spirit within me" (Ps. 51:10). David was a warrior, a general, a king, a world diplomat. But David was a man with an impure heart. He held grudges. He used violence. He accumulated wives. David's heart was not always pure.

David knew his heart was impure. He knew that he could not, by his own power, set his heart right. He couldn't purge the evil and daily renew his steadfastness. David needed God. Without God everything else in David's life, even his heart, would be rendered babble—senseless and meaningless. So David prayed, "God, please, clean my heart, and give me a spirit of faithfulness."

"Who can say, 'I have kept my heart pure; I am clean and without sin?'" David knew he couldn't. But he knew that God could clean his heart and conscience for him. He will do it for us, too, when we pray, "Create in me a pure heart, O God."

MORTAL COMBAT

Make plans by seeking advice; if you wage war, obtain guidance.
—Proverbs 20:18

The armies numbered in the tens of millions with tens of thousands of tanks and planes. Each side was determined to wipe out the other. Few military operations in history generate more interest than the war between Germany and Russia.

For a time both sides practiced a policy of no retreat. They would stand and fight for hours, even days, nonstop, no sleep, no dinner breaks, just shooting round-the-clock. The Russians even had lines of soldiers behind the front line troops. If any troops retreated they were shot by their fellow Russians positioned behind them. German armies occasionally found thousands of Russian bodies that they didn't kill; they were mowed down by their own soldiers when they tried to retreat. The Russians even welded the doors of the tanks shut, trapping their soldiers within. There would be no use in retreating. Their only option was to plunge ahead into the German lines.

Can you imagine how brutal such a policy was? No retreat. No withdrawal. In the end that policy hurt both sides. The Germans lost hundreds of thousands of troops they might not have lost if they would have allowed retreating and regrouping; the Russians lost millions. Neither side showed very much concern for their own troops. The Russians often left their own wounded on the battlefield to fend for themselves.

The war between Germany and Russia was mortal combat such as the world had never seen. In the end both sides counted their casualties in the millions. It was a no-holds-barred, all-out, conquer-or-be-conquered, winner-take-all drama. Can you see why this war continues to generate interest?

This war interests me for another reason. I see it as a type for the kind of war we are in, those of us who believe in good and evil, light and darkness, heaven and hell. We are in a no-holds-barred, all-out, conquer-or-be-conquered, winner-take-all drama. No quarter is given by the enemy. Losers face a prisoner-of-war camp; the Bible calls it a lake of burning sulphur for the devil and his army (Matt. 25:41).

There is no retreating in this war either. Jesus said that no man who looks back is fit for the plow. We forge ahead. In Matthew 16 he said we storm the gates of hell. We are an army on the march.

I know this makes it sound pretty dramatic. It is. Even though we may not always be conscious of the war we are in, God is always aware. The devil is also always aware. The battle cost the life of Jesus. It may cost you yours, but it doesn't have to. Jesus lived and died to free us from the power of the evil one. "You shall know the truth, and the truth will set you free" (John 8:32).

"Make plans by seeking advice; if you wage war, obtain guidance." Fortunately, in this spiritual war we are in, we have advice and guidance from the Lord himself. As long as we continue to fight on the side of he who is "the way, the truth and the life," we will have victory.

TEMPTATIONS OF THE RIGHTEOUS

He who pursues righteousness and love finds life, prosperity and honor.

—Proverbs 21:21

Scripture promises big things for those who pursue righteousness: life, prosperity, and honor. There is more. Another proverb says, "The Lord's curse is on the house of the wicked, but he blesses the home of the righteous" (Prov. 3:33). Righteousness is the way to go. God curses the wicked but blesses the righteous and all who dwell in covenant with him. Righteousness wins out over wickedness.

So how do we become righteous? When we say, "Okay, we're righteous now, Lord, start blessing us," haven't we already lost what we have been seeking? What does it take to be righteous?

In the Old Testament righteousness was understood as living within the "two-way relationship between God and man . . . the righteousness of God appears in his God-like dealings with his people, i.e., in redemption and salvation" (Dictionary of New Testament Theology [Grand Rapids: Zondervan, 1979], 3:355). In other words, because God is good and righteous, he allows man to live in relation with him. That is what allows a man to be considered righteous. Isaiah 56:1–2 says, "This is what the Lord says: maintain justice and do what is right, for my salvation is close at hand and my righteousness will soon be revealed. Blessed is the man who does this, the man who holds it fast. " A righteous man in the Old Testament lived in relationship with God and tried to live his life in a way that reflected the nature of God—doing what is just and right.

The New Testament says that our righteousness today is because of Jesus Christ: "God made him (Jesus) who had no sin to be sin for us, so that in him we might become the righteousness of God" (2 Cor. 5:21). Romans 4:24 says God will credit righteousness to those who believe in God.

The Sage didn't have this New Testament idea of righteousness. For him righteousness was understood as living within the covenant of God and reflecting the character of God in his lifestyle—truth, goodness, justice, integrity, honesty, humility, forgiveness, and love. Solomon said that the person who reflected this lifestyle would be richly blessed in all the ways named above. Blessed is the man who is righteous! But here is a caution to those who seek God's righteousness: there are certain temptations to those who would be righteous.

One temptation is pride. We can feel pride that we are following God, that we know the Word, that we worship regularly. Pride is the opposite of righteousness since it does not reflect the love of God and humble disposition to others. The presence of pride may well reflect another temptation of righteousness: blindness.

Those pursuing righteousness need to caution against being blind to their own failings and sins. A heart ready to confess, "I have sinned" (1 John 1:9), reveals a heart that is still sensitive. But pride can cause our blindness—an unwillingness to see and admit our faults. But there is another temptation that can prevent us from seeing and admitting our pride: hypocrisy.

Hypocrisy is the setting of our own standards of righteousness. Worshiping on Sunday but lying on Monday is not righteousness. Saying a prayer before a meal but then gossiping during the meal is not righteousness. Our standard may justify such behavior, but it is God's righteousness we are pursuing!

"He who pursues righteousness and love finds life, prosperity and honor" is still true. Jesus added that those pursuing righteousness would be blessed (Matt. 5:6). Remember these important dispositions of heart in pursuit of God's righteousness: humility, openness to our own sins, and the honesty to say, "I have sinned." This kind of righteousness is what God seeks in us, and he will bless us with life, prosperity, and honor.

ONE EASILY ANGERED

Do not make friends with a hot-tempered man, do not associate with one easily angered.

—Proverbs 22:24

This verse makes me think of grizzly bears. There are things I don't particularly like about grizzlies. They will occasionally crash a party and show up at dinner uninvited. Actually they take the whole dinner and run the hosts away. Grizzly bears have learned to run toward the sounds of gunshots because it means there is an elk or deer lying on the ground. Mr. Grizzly charges upon the scene and chases off the hunter, keeping the whole meal for himself.

I also don't like how grizzlies chew on people. They chew on your arms, your legs, even your head. If you have ever seen anyone who had an encounter with a grizzly like that, they wear scars.

Thirdly, I resent that these huge critters practice horrible oral hygiene. They never brush their teeth. Never. People who have been attacked by bears say what they remembered most about the experience was the horrible, disgusting breath of the big brute. Grizzlies eat rotten meat and garbage, and they've never been introduced to breath mints.

For all of these negative aspects of grizzly bears, they are incredible creatures: powerful, hostile, destructive, fearless. They are the king of the forest. I actually have a lot of respect for them, even something of a fascination. But I still don't want to meet up with one close and personal. I have been in grizzly country. My senses were on high alert the whole time. Every branch that creaked made me startle. Every twig that snapped made me snap. After a short time of that intensity, the muscles in my neck stiffened and my back and shoulders grew weary from rapidly turning and looking for the big bruin.

I respect those animals for their strength, power, and potential destructiveness. But I don't want to meet one for those very reasons.

The Sage says the same thing about an angry man. An angry man is like a grizzly bear—he can become powerful. He can become fearless and destructive. The path of this angry man is strewn with hurt and broken lives, the victims of his tantrums.

I've seen women with bruises on their faces from the wrath of their own two-legged grizzly, their husbands or boyfriends. I've seen young men cower in fear in the presence of any adult male, their fear the result of years of living in the dark shadows of an abusive father. I have visited young men in prison who were too weak to resist the lead of an angry mentor who led his young charge into crime. I've visited with fathers who were seeking help for their children—emotionally scarred from years of malicious scolding received from the fury of their mothers.

The Sage knew what he was talking about when he said, "Do not make friends with a hot-tempered man, do not associate with one easily angered." The next verse says, "or you may learn his ways and get yourself ensnared." Here is the reason: like a stirred-up grizzly, the angry man will hurt you. He will either drag you into his destructive behavior, or he will vent his anger upon you. Either way, you lose.

The Sage had even more to say about anger: "Anger is cruel and fury overwhelming" (Prov. 26:4). Sounds a bit like a grizzly, doesn't it? "A fool gives full vent to his anger" (Prov. 29:11). So stay out of an angry man's way. "An angry man stirs up dissension, and a hot-tempered one commits many sins" (Prov. 29:22). One of those sins may be his abuse of you.

"Do not make friends with a hot-tempered man, do not associate with one easily angered." Good advice, advice intended to keep you safe.

GLAD HEART

> My son, if your heart is wise, then my heart will be glad; my inmost being will rejoice when your lips speak what is right.
> —Proverbs 23:15–16

"I'm sorry, Dad."

"What for?"

"For moving the grandchildren so faraway."

Is there any grandparent who does not know the desperate longing of seeing and holding grandchildren who live many hours away? Spoiling the kids is a grandparents' privilege. But how can grandma and grandpa do their job when their grandchildren live twenty hours away?

Sometimes my mom would look at the pictures of her grandchildren on the wall and cry. She longed to hold them and hug them. Grandma lived in Tennessee; her grandchildren lived in Texas, Wyoming, and Montana.

So I apologized to Dad for that one time. He said, "You have nothing to feel sorry about. We don't care where you decide to live or what you decide to do, so long as you live a good life. All we ask of all you kids is that you live good lives."

"Live good lives." I think that is what Solomon had in mind when he told his son, "If your heart is wise, then my heart will be glad."

Every healthy mother and father wants what is best for their children. They want them to fit in, do well in school, have stylish clothing, get into a good college, and land a job that will enable them to pay their school loans. Those are all worthy desires for our children.

Solomon, though, takes the concern a step further. "What matters most to me, son, is that your heart is wise. I want to see the seeds of honesty, purity, and integrity take root in your heart. I want to see the fruit of these virtues blossom into modest behavior and speech. Son, it doesn't matter that you climb to the top of the ladder in your profession or that you receive acclaim for social accomplishments, if you are unkind, selfish, or foolish. You will break our hearts if you achieve success at the cost of character development. Make us happy by showing a wisdom that transcends the approval of cheering crowds and is molded by the approval of God."

That is what my dad told me. "Live a good life. That is what will make your mom and me happiest."

I understand that now. My children are about all grown. One is out of college, one is in college and another is in high school. I want them to do well in school, attract the attention of a prospective employer, and get a job that will pay their bills and assure their retirement. But that is not what I want most for them. I want them to live good lives. My heart and my wife's heart will rejoice only if our children are wise in speech and behavior.

Wise in Proverbs does not mean smart. Wise means to be shaped by God. The wise person feeds upon the Word of God, and this nutrition strengthens the muscles and sinews of his character. "Apply your heart to instruction and your ears to words of knowledge," Solomon advises (Prov. 23:12).

The heart open to instruction has hope of becoming wise. A wise heart looks beyond the joys and sorrows, the victories and defeat of this age to the all-surpassing glory of the age to come. In that age we will all be together, family and friends, grandparents and their grandchildren, the wise and their God.

I would like to have my children and grandchildren live close to me in my last years. I'd like to go to their ball games, show them how to raise a garden, and be there for Christmas. But even more important, I want them to live good lives because if they do, if we do, I will see them again on the other side. That will make my heart truly glad.

A LYING TONGUE

A lying tongue hates those it hurts.
—Proverbs 26:28a

Proverbs says the liar hates people, especially the one he is lying to. That is a strong accusation. I think of a liar as someone out to save his own neck. He gets caught in a dirty deed, or he is about to get caught, so he lies to escape exposure and to escape trouble. I think of a liar as being extremely self-centered.

He is. But the extent of his self-centeredness may escape us. In telling lies, the Sage says the liar hates other people. It is not just a matter of saving his own skin. Rather, the liar is skinning the one he is lying to. Love and respect produce honesty. If your bad deed is about to be uncovered by one you love and respect, won't those positive attitudes toward that person make you tell them the truth? Love and respect produce truth and trust. Why would you lie unless you were so self-centered that saving your own skin meant more to you than being honest to the one you supposedly love? Your lie reveals a dark side of your heart and shows that your love is not genuine enough to risk the truth. You prefer painting a rosy picture and misleading the person you supposedly love rather than being honest with them. The bottom line is you don't really love them. Your lie is a child of your hate.

"A lying tongue hates those it hurts." But there is another truth about a liar. A lying tongue hurts other people. That is further evidence of the self-centeredness of the liar. "If I get caught, I'm going to get it in the neck," the liar reasons. "But why should I get hurt? I'll stick it to someone else." Thus his lie is born, and someone will be hurt.

Liars hate people. Liars hurt people. I think that is why elsewhere in Proverbs the Sage wrote, "The Lord detests (hates) lying lips" (Prov. 12:22). The Lord hates lying lips because they hate and they hurt. God is about love and comfort. Everything a liar does works against what God tries to do.

Ultimately, what God wants to do with the love and comfort he offers is to enjoy the company of his people in holy community; and he wants us to enjoy that company as well. To secure this kind of community, God uses love and truth. Indeed, to show his desire for community, God sent his own son Jesus. Jesus describes his work and ministry in building community this way: "I am the way and the truth and the life. No one comes to the Father except through me" (John 14:6). Jesus came in love (John 3:16), and he told the truth; but even more than that, Jesus embodied truth. Just as God can not lie or bear lies neither can Jesus (Heb. 6:18). Jesus is truth, the truth of God.

Truth is sometimes difficult and hard. Think of Peter announcing the truth to Ananias and Sapphira. When they lied about their contribution to the Lord, Peter told them the truth: "You have not lied to men but to God" (Acts 5:4). As a consequence of their lies, Ananias and Sapphira were punished with death.

We might have counseled with Ananias and Sapphira, trying to bring about repentance. "Look, guys, you know you shouldn't lie." Not Peter. He just announced their sentence: "You're dead." He knows that liars hate and hurt, and with their lies they disrupt community. He knows that God hates lying lips. For Peter, as for God, there is no coddling for liars.

Will Willimon says, "Sometimes the truth hurts. Here, it kills. But lies are the death of community—at least a community that hopes to be a prophetic community of truthfulness in service to the Lord who is the Way, the Life, and the Truth" (Pastor, 276). If a lying tongue hates those it hurts, a truthful tongue must love those it nurtures. It certainly contributes to the building of a community where God can dwell in love and truth with his people.

COMMUNITY

THE NEXT WAR

A scoundrel and villain, who goes about with a corrupt mouth . . .
who plots evil with deceit in his heart—he always stirs up
dissension. Therefore disaster will overtake him in an instant; he
will suddenly be destroyed—without remedy.

—Proverbs 6:12–15

The movie To End All Wars (2001) is about a group of British soldiers in a Japanese POW camp during World War II. Their existence is grim and hopeless. The men are "living to die" as one narrated line informs the viewer.

In one scene a number of the hapless British prisoners are lying around daydreaming of when the war will be over. They can only dream, only fantasize, that they will outlive the torture, the starvation rations, the forced work on the railroad, and make it home alive and healthy enough to enjoy life afterward.

"What are you going to do when you get out?" one soldier asked. "I'm going to enjoy the loving arms of my wife," another answered.

"What are you going to do when you get out?" "I'm going to get into black market crime and make a ton of money. I'm going to get rich!"

One more POW is asked, "What are you going to do when you get out?" He answers, "I'm going to start preparing for the next war."

With this last answer the men were slapped back into reality. All conversation ceased. A moment of heavy silence followed, and then the movie graciously switched scenes. There will be another war. There will be more discord.

Proverbs says, "The unfaithful have a craving for violence" (Prov. 13:2). Such people are perverse. They have no regard for community, for healthy relationships, for getting along with others, for leading a character-based lifestyle themselves, or for leading others to one. They glory in discord, trouble, violence. They are very intentional in their approach to causing trouble. "A violent man entices his neighbor and leads him down a path that is not good" (Prov. 16:29).

Are violent men just ignorant? Are they unaware of the trouble they cause themselves and others? Not according to the Wisdom tradition. Violent people know the trouble they cause; they do it on purpose, and they lead others into it as well.

Violent people are serious disturbers of community. They hurt people. They rob them of joy. They deprive them of hope. These violent disturbers may be local criminals working solo, or they may be abusive guards in a prison camp working in cahoots with others. But one thing they have in common: they ruin lives.

We have police departments and a legal system to deal with the violent, but they will always be with us. What are we going to do about it? Start preparing for the next war?

At the end of the movie To End All Wars, one of the British POWs beats a Japanese officer who himself was abusive to the prisoners. The POW is seeking revenge. Do you blame him? But another British hero tries to stop the revenge abuse and says, "War is the final destination of hatred." His point: get rid of the hatred.

It may seem that we are helpless in the presence of violence, but we can do this: we can maintain our own character. We can promote peace. We can manifest the spirit of the cross in our lives. We can remember that those who pursue peace will one day reap the reward of their work. It is the peacemakers who will hear God's blessing, "You are sons of God" (Matt. 5:9).

DISCIPLINE FOR LIFE

He who heeds discipline shows the way to life, but whoever ignores correction leads others astray.

—Proverbs 10:17

I don't care very much for discipline, at least not the corrective or punitive kind. Discipline is hard on the emotions. When you are a kid it can be tough on the nerve endings, too.

We are accustomed to the idea of children being disciplined, but adults? Do we still need to be rebuked or corrected as adults, or do we outgrow the need for discipline? What value is there in being disciplined anyway? I can think of one man who has some interesting stories of discipline to tell.

Jesus asked this man, "Who do people say the Son of Man is?" The man answered, "You are the Christ, the Son of the living God" to which Jesus replied, "Blessed are you . . . for this was not revealed to you by man, but by my Father in heaven" (Matt. 16:13, 16–17). In the very next story Jesus explains to his disciples that he is going to suffer and die. This same man objects and rebukes Jesus, saying, "Never, Lord! This shall never happen to you!" Jesus then corrects him with a stern rebuke: "Get behind me, Satan!" (Matt. 16:21–23). How is it that the same disciple can receive praise from Jesus for speaking the revealed truth of God, and in the next story be called "Satan" by Jesus? It happened because Peter lacked understanding about who Jesus was and what his mission was about. Jesus explained to him, "You are a stumbling block to me; you do not have in mind the things of God, but the things of men" (Matt. 16:23). This man needed correction and discipline because he lacked understanding and maturity, and his ignorance carried the potential of harming the work of Christ.

The story of his discipline doesn't end here with this rebuke from Jesus. Later he was rebuked by another Christian, the apostle Paul. It happened in Antioch when this man was enjoying fellowship in the church with Gentile Christians. He worshiped with them, visited with them, even ate with them. Then some Jewish Christians showed up. Even though they were all Christians the old ethnic tension between Jews and Gentiles raised its ugly head. The man, a preacher now, withdrew his fellowship from his Gentile brothers. Paul was there and said, "Brother, you are wrong. You are acting hypocritically" (Gal. 2:11–13; Gallagher, At the Altar, pp. 231–33).

Who is this man? He was an early follower of Jesus. He spent three years with him on a personal basis. He was also an apostle and preached the first gospel sermon after Jesus' resurrection. He was an early missionary. He was the author of two letters in the New Testament. His life was incredibly important to the early church and continues to be of major importance to the church today. He was the apostle Peter.

Not even one so close to Jesus, one personally schooled by Jesus, was exempt from the Lord's discipline, administered either by Jesus himself or another Christian. Peter himself could not escape rebuke. It is good that Peter listened, learned, and continued to follow. "He who heeds discipline shows the way to life." Peter is able to show us the way to life, even today, because he heeded the way of discipline.

Discipline continues to be tough and always will be. But offered in the proper spirit by a loving brother, discipline can be lifesaving. "Do not despise the Lord's discipline and do not resent his rebuke because the Lord disciplines those he loves, as a father the son he delights in" (Prov. 3:11–12). Correction and rebuke is not fun, but it is the way to life for those who open their hearts to God's ongoing work in their lives.

A KIND MAN

A kind man benefits himself, but a cruel man brings trouble on himself.

—Proverbs 11:17

As a kid I remember strangers knocking on our door in the country. City folks, many of them. They were usually lost, out of gas, or broken down. Mom and Dad always helped them with a few gallons of fuel or some makeshift repair on their automobile. I even remember one couple whose care broke down staying at our house all night. In all those years I never remember my parents taking any of the money that was offered to them for the help, service, or gasoline they gave. Never.

"Here, take a few bucks for the gas," someone would offer.

"No," Dad would say. "I'm just glad you appreciate it. But if you want to pay me back, next time you see someone broken down or in need of assistance, help them. That is how you can pay me back." A kind man benefits himself, but a cruel man brings trouble on himself.

A kind man benefits himself . . . maybe a man like Abraham? Abraham had his character flaws, but he also had his character strengths. Remember when his nephew Lot was captured in battle? Forsaking his own safety, Abraham raised a band of men and went after Lot to rescue him. Even earlier, when Lot's herds and Abraham's herds grew too large for the land to support them, Abraham unselfishly allowed Lot to select the land he would like to move into. That was kindness.

That kindness paid off for Abraham. He was richly blessed by God. That's not to say, of course, that every time we do something nice for someone we can expect a flood of blessings from heaven in reciprocation. As Christians we have already received an abundance of blessings from heaven, including our redemption. But in a general way acts of kindness tend to generate other acts of kindness, and at least sometimes, they indeed come back to us. A kind man benefits himself.

A cruel man brings trouble on himself . . . maybe a man like Ahab? Ahab was the king who wanted the vineyard of Naboth. Naboth was living on land he inherited from his ancestors though, and he wasn't willing to sell it to the king. Ahab's wife, Jezebel, wasn't one to let a simple citizen disappoint the aspirations of a king! She conspired with some scoundrels to frame Naboth on trumped-up charges leading to his execution. Ahab was a cruel man who was later killed in battle. Jezebel was a cruel woman who was later thrown to her death from an upper-story window. A cruel man brings trouble on himself.

A proverb is a truism or principle. A proverb should not be thought of as a rule that always works itself out in the same way in every circumstance. It is a principle that says, "In general, this is a statement that reflects experience in life."

Somewhere in the Sage's life he experienced this truism: "A kind man benefits himself, but a cruel man brings trouble on himself." Perhaps it was a kindness passed on to him he consciously passed on to another who passed it on to another who . . . well, you get the point. Whether it is sharing gasoline with a stranger knocking at your door or sharing food with a hungry child across the street, acts of kindness have a life of their own that keep on living and enriching the lives of others.

In my travels, especially as a college student driving old cars, I have been the recipient of a kind gentleman stopping to offer a hand to a kid who looked like he was in trouble. At times, I've offered a few bucks as a thank you. I've heard these words echoed from my childhood: "If you want to pay me back, next time you see someone broken down or in need of assistance, help them. That is how you can pay me back."

HOUSE OF THE RIGHTEOUS

Wicked men are overthrown and are no more, but the house of the righteous stands firm.

—Proverbs 12:7

"Misery loves company." I heard that saying as a kid whenever I was in trouble or would pout. We don't like being alone in our discomfort or self-pity. Misery loves company.

But that saying is true only to a point. Misery can get bad enough that, even though we want others to join us, no one will. The price is too high. The underage drinking crowd thinks they're having a blast until the police arrive, then buddies run for cover or rat on each other in hopes of a lighter sentence. As the misery increases, the friendship tends to decrease.

That may be why Proverbs says, "The wicked are overthrown." God may be the one who intervenes and overthrows them. Then again the wicked may overthrow themselves. Years of wild behavior, irresponsible living, criminal activity, and abusive treatment of others takes a toll on people. No one wants to be around them. They do themselves in. Loneliness is their lot. They have no family, no belonging, no community.

But it is different with the righteous. "The house of the righteous stands firm" and the righteous endure. Why is that? Because of the nature of the house, or the family, of the righteous.

In ancient Israel "the household was a common setting for the issuance of wisdom in the form of the teachings of the parents to their children. In addition, the moral life often dealt with issues common to the household. The household in ancient Israel . . . was an extended social unit that lineally included multiple generations (grandparents, parents, and children) and laterally to include aunts, uncles, and cousins" (Leo G. Perdue, Proverbs: Interpretation [Louisville: John Knox Press, 2000], p. 169). All of these family members influenced the children.

The wicked man likes the company of other wicked people in his bad behavior (see Proverbs 1:8–19). He has a "gang" mentality and recruits people to participate in evil with him. Eventually his evil behavior separates him from upstanding citizens and he is left alone with his gang. In time even his association with other wicked or criminal people can play out, as loneliness, prison, and even death isolates him from others (Prov. 1:19). His own behavior separates him from meaningful and supportive community, even that of his own family.

But the righteous man has his family. The very nature of the ancient godly household and of a godly household today means that we always have people around us who are supportive and offer accountability. A youngster in such a close family is taught right and wrong by his parents. However, he also has grandparents, aunts, and uncles, and even older siblings and cousins who are there to help shape his behavior, offer good advice, and even offer correction.

"It takes a village to raise a child." For the Christian today that village is the family. Here we are taught wisdom and see wisdom manifested in the lives of the older people. Here we are held accountable if we wander from the ways of wisdom to act irresponsibly or rebelliously. This village also encompasses extended family. If we live far away from extended family then the church assumes that role. Relationships we build at church are not just for our social pleasure. They fulfill the ancient purpose of God for the extended relationships that help us by passing on wisdom, solid character, and good behavior to our children.

"Wicked men are overthrown and are no more, but the house of the righteous stands firm." The house of the righteous stands firm because it is built on the ancient principles of godly living and family interaction.

THE HANDSHAKE THAT COULD HAVE BEEN

> From the fruit of his lips a man is filled with good things as surely
> as the work of his hands rewards him.
>   —Proverbs 12:14

In October 1529 several Reformation greats met at Marburg, Germany, to discuss important points of biblical doctrine. Luther, Zwingli, and others were present; and together they hammered out an agreement on fourteen important points of doctrine, including the Trinity, original sin, faith, and justification. One topic of discussion, the fifteenth one, almost reached total agreement: the Lord's Supper. There were five points of agreement on the Lord's Supper and one point of disagreement. That singular point was on how to understand the presence of Christ in the observance of the supper. Was Christ present in some actual, physical way in the bread and wine? Was he present in spirit? Or was his presence only represented by the emblems?

Zwingli maintained that Christ's body can only be physically present in one place at one time, and right now he is at the right hand of God. Therefore, he is present at our observance of the Lord's Supper in a spiritual, but not physical, way. The bread and wine do not become literal body and bread—they are signs that "signify" or point to the Christ.

Luther maintained the real presence of Christ in the supper. Luther rejected transubstantiation—the view that the emblems became the actual body and blood of Jesus—but he did argue for some sense of the real, physical presence of Christ. Agreement could not be reached on this point. These scholars reached agreement on 14 5/6 of the items they were discussing but failed to reach a consensus on this last one: how to understand the presence of Christ at the table.

It shouldn't have been a big deal, right? That's what Zwingli thought. With tears in his eyes, he extended his hand to Martin Luther. It was a handshake of acceptance, of esteem for Luther's scholarship and ministry, and of brotherliness. But Luther refused Zwingli's hand. "You have a different spirit," Luther told Zwingli. This ended the meeting of the reformers, and it scuttled the effectiveness of future reunion meetings (Donald K. McKim, Theological Turning Points: Major Issues in Christian Thought [Atlanta: John Knox Press, 1988], p. 144–46).

The handshake that could have been. A handshake that could have united reformation and restoration efforts four hundred years ago. A handshake that could have fostered brotherly attitudes and kept men with similar intentions working together instead of apart. A handshake that could have brought rewards of good things. A handshake that could have, I believe, avoided a number of costly wars in Europe over several generations, costly in terms of dollars and human life. But that handshake didn't happen.

It's ironic how gifts God gives us for unity and brotherliness actually accomplish the opposite of what he intends. In marriage, for example, the gifts of communication and intimacy are to be unifying elements in the marriage. Failure to exercise them properly, however, sends many couples to counselors and sometimes to divorce courts. In the church the gift of the Lord's Supper, intended by God to be a unifying element among brothers, serves as a point of contention and even division. Zwingli and Luther serve as only one example of God's good intentions gone awry.

God gave us the Lord's Supper to orient us to Christ, to one another, and to the banquet we will one day enjoy with him. Through the supper God extends to us his right hand of fellowship. I hope as believers we always extend ours to one another, sharing God's presence through his meal.

BITTERNESS

Each heart knows its own bitterness.
—Proverbs 14:10

The porch was his home. He slept in the house, but early in the day he limped to the porch. Here he sat for most of the day, eating lunch, drinking iced tea, and smoking. Oh, and rocking in his chair. This was his life. I spent part of an afternoon with him on that porch in the summer of 1977 when I was selling books for the Southwestern Company. My work took me to this porch and this man.

Anger and bitterness oozed from this man' pores. When he talked, his eyes would squint. As his story came out, he rocked faster and smoked more intensely. Old feelings came up that he had never laid to rest.

I guessed him to be about forty-five years old. Since I was only eighteen at the time, forty-five seemed old. But he seemed more like seventy. His body was thin and frail. His fingers were curled at weird angles, so the smoke from his cigarette singed them. They were horribly discolored. I knew this man had a story, and I was anxious to hear it.

This man and his wife had a tumultuous relationship. He suspected her of stepping out on him, so he confronted her. A terrible fight ensued and he felt hurt and rejected. He stormed out of the house, got into his car, and raced away. He was in a highly irritated state, unable to control either himself or his car. He failed to navigate a turn, smashed into a telephone pole, and broke his neck. While he was in traction in the hospital, his wife made her official break and left him for her boyfriend.

The man recovered enough to regain some semblance of a life. He could shuffle along and use his hands. Arthritis crippled him now even more severely than the neck injury had, but neither the broken neck nor the arthritis caused the most devastating handicap for this man. No, his real handicap came from the bitterness and resentment that accompanied his broken heart.

"Can you believe it? She left me while I was in the hospital! Couldn't she have waited until I got out of the hospital to leave me? Why did she have to bolt and chase some other guy when I needed her the most!"

That was a heavy afternoon for this teenager. I didn't pretend to know what to tell him. I hurt for him, but that didn't help him. Besides, he had hurt enough for himself. Over all those years of his stewing about the past, reliving the fights, mentally reenacting his escape in the car, the wreck, the hospital, and the faithlessness of his wife, over all those years the man became so accustomed to his hurt, anger, and bitterness that now he couldn't see any other way to live. Bitterness took root so deeply in his heart that it caused greater damage than a broken neck or arthritis ever could.

Maybe I was naive but, I left there resolving in my mind to never let any experience in life, no matter how devastating, leave me as broken inside as this man. I was only eighteen and full of youthful hope and promise but, I believed God could somehow provide comfort no matter how serious a tragedy I might experience.

Through the years I have frequently wondered about this man. Did he have a mom and dad who still loved him? A brother or sister? A church family? A relationship with Christ? No, none of them can take the place of a spouse that we love, but they can function as ministers of the grace and mercy of God. They can offer hope and encouragement. "A happy heart makes the face cheerful, but heartache crushes the spirit" (Prov. 15:13).

I've never been as hurt as this man. By faith I have to trust in the promises of God that there is a peace that passes all understanding (Phil. 4:7). One day I'm sure my faith will be put to the test. My hope is that my family, Christian friends and faith will sustain me the way God promises they can.

I wanted to share all this on the porch that day. But the man had bitterness and anger as his companions and wouldn't make room for any others. He felt he had no choice. But the fact is, we do have a choice. We can choose today to have a heart of faith, hope, trust and yes, even forgiveness, by God's abundant grace and mercy.

OVERLOOKING OFFENSES

"A man's wisdom gives him patience; it is to his glory to overlook an offense."

Proverbs 19:11

Wisdom is skill at living. Just as people have skill in carpentry, sports or music, people can have skill in living. A good life is not the product of luck or genetics; it is the product of studying life, just as people study a trade. To be wise is to be a craftsmen skilled in the art of making good choices, maintaining healthy relationships, and living faithfully for God.

One way we know if we are gaining mastery in the art of living well is by how we respond to insults, putdowns and other offenses. A normal response to an offense is to respond in kind. If someone attacks our work or family, it is natural to reach into our arsenal of verbal weapons and counterattack. Insults, putdowns, and mocking humor are effective implements of war to turn against our verbal assailant. Such weapons may be effective, but they also are counterproductive to becoming the kind of person God calls us to be: wise.

Proverbs says that one hallmark of wisdom is patience: "A man's wisdom gives him patience." Patience is the ability to restrain one's impulse rather than lash out; it is the discipline to check one's emotions rather than vent them. A fool speaks the first thing that comes to his mind, whether it is healthy or sick. His mouth gushes with folly (Proverbs 15:2) and is quick to take up a quarrel (Proverbs 20:3). There is no wisdom in the heart of a fool, so there is no knowledge on his lips, either (Proverbs 14:7).

The wise man has learned that it is best to settle his emotions and restrain his words. He avoids heightening the quarrel and rupturing relationships. Even if his feelings are hurt, he swallows his pride long enough to settle down. He may still choose to confront his attacker, but he will do it when the hostility is diffused and the conversation is calm.

I have to admit, this is not easy to do! When attacked, I want to attack back. When insulted, I want to show that I, too, can engage. Yet when I do, Proverbs says I am not being wise. When I give in to the intensity of my emotions, I allow my baser instincts to prevail over my better judgment.

Proverbs places a high premium on the ability to hold one's emotions and tongue in line: "It is to his glory to overlook an offense." We think it is glorious to attack our attacker and defeat him in the game of verbal abuse. That is true only if we are foolish. How many families and friendships have been permanently marred because someone wouldn't be wise enough to be quiet?

It is hard to overlook an offense. It takes the skill of a craftsman to master emotions. Not everyone can or will do it. Only the wise will. But here is an incentive to pray for the ability and to put forth the effort to learn to be patient and overlook an offense: It's what God does. Micah says of God, "You do not stay angry forever, but delight to show mercy" (Micah 7:18b).

I tell the following story with shame. I was engaged with another disgruntled person in bad-mouthing a mutual friend when that friend walked into the room. Our sudden silence and stunned expressions had to alert him that he was the subject of our conversation. He just smiled, looked at each of us, and asked, "So what's going on?" He gave us an out. I'll never forget that moment and the grace my friend showed us by letting us off the hook. He refused to respond to an offense with an offense. "A man's wisdom gives him patience; it is to his glory to overlook an offense." My friend's delight in showing mercy saved a friendship and provided me a glimpse of the greatness and glory of God.

WHAT IS DESIRABLE IN A MAN

What is desirable in a man is his kindness, and it is better to be
a poor man than a liar.

—Proverbs 19:22 (NASB)

Is kindness a desirable trait? It depends on what you are looking for.
If you are a football coach, you may not care if one of your players says
"thank you" to the waitress or if he smiles politely when he signs autographs.
What you desire in this man is that he can move the football ten yards, then
another ten yards. Speed, determination, drive, even a degree of ruthlessness
are what you desire in this man. But kindness?

The Hebrew word for kindness is hesed. Hesed means steadfast love
or kindness. We know that the world values many qualities above love or
kindness. Do we care if our stockbroker is a loving man who hugs his children
when he goes home at night? Or do we care more that he can turn a profit
for us? Do we esteem love or kindness in a boxer? Think how that can mess
a match up if a boxer pauses to apologize to his opponent for hurting him
with a vicious right. "I love you, man. Here, let me help you up."

However, God values love and kindness. My three kids value love and
kindness in their dad. My wife does in her husband. When I don't treat
them with love and kindness, I hurt them.

Hesed also means loyalty. Loyalty is the quality of hanging in there with
someone through thick and thin. "A friend loves at all times, and a brother
is born for adversity" (Prov. 17:17). "There is a friend who sticks closer than
a brother" (Prov. 18:24).

Proverbs says, "These qualities are what God is looking for in a man. Others
may value professional ability or athletic skill; but to build a quality life, a man
needs love, kindness, and loyalty. I'd rather you be a poor man with godly
character than a rich man with a success-at-any-cost mentality. Using worldly
techniques may help you achieve a level of success that will get you in a popular
magazine, but you will not become the kind of man I am looking for."

I'm thinking of a man's life based on this quality of hesed: love, kindness,
and loyalty. This man never owned a house. He was never elected mayor and
was never the "Citizen of the Year." His investment portfolio was . . . well,
it wasn't. He didn't have one. Worldly achievement was not very important
to him.

Instead, he spent his life investing in the lives of others. He was a caregiver to the sick. He grieveded with mourners and wept with the brokenhearted. He stopped along the trail to pat a child on the head and even stooped to give a hug. He defended the defenseless against the religious and civic power brokers of his day, placing himself in jeopardy for doing so.

This man exhibited all the qualities of hesed, but what did he have to show for it toward the end of his days? "The Son of man has no place to lay his head" (Matt. 8:20). The world may not value hesed. But God does. That is why, today, even after the world rejected Jesus, his Father honors him as the glorified Son: resurrected, ascended, and in the presence of the Father.

What is desirable in a man is his kindness, his love, his loyalty. God desires those qualities. Your wife does too, your husband, children, parents, and friends. The world might even begin to value them if it sees hesed demonstrated in your life.

CRAVING EVIL

The wicked man craves evil; his neighbor gets no mercy from him.
—Proverbs 21:10

The "rugged individualist" was the fearless soul who braved the dangers of nineteenth-century America and moved west. The rugged individualist lived by himself and conquered the native inhabitants, grizzly bears, dry summers, and cold winters, all by himself. He didn't need anybody!

There is some truth to that, but only some. Even in those harsh "olden days," people needed people. Barn raisings, harvest, and the birth of a baby drew neighbors together to help. Even in the days of the Wild West and the untamed frontier, people still sought out other people. They needed community.

John Donne wrote, "No man is an island . . . I am involved in mankind." (Meditation VXII). This idea is emphasized in Proverbs. "The wicked man craves evil; his neighbor gets no mercy from him."

Wherever people go, they crave and create community. It is easier to live with other people, even with their rough edges, than it is to live all alone.

However, there are people who crave something other than community. Some people crave only what they selfishly desire. Their own pursuits become primary, even if it wreaks havoc in the community of faith or family. They simply don't care about anything other than what they want. "One can allow a desire or appetite to gain such control that it takes over a person's whole life" (Bland, Proverbs, p. 192). Consider Amnon's attack of Tamar (2 Sam. 13:1–19) and Samson's unholy hunger for the women of Philistia (Judg. 14 and 16). Both Amnon and Samson disregarded the good of the larger community—their family and Israel—to the detriment of themselves and the people they hurt. "The wicked man craves evil; his neighbor gets no mercy from him."

Who is the wicked man? One who craves evil (Prov. 21:10). What is his evil? Selfishness. The evil man thinks only of himself and craves what he wants. He disregards his neighbor, a member of his community. That neighbor might be his wife and kids, people at his church, the guy he works with, or the man who lives next door. This guy just doesn't care about the needs of others. He shows no respect or concern for others. That, to the Sage, is his great sin—he lives to himself. No mercy for his neighbors, no kindness, no consideration.

The evil man's offenses are not necessarily great ones. Maybe a guy just turned his radio up too loud. Perhaps he peeks in his neighbor's window. He might be rude to the waitress. Whatever his offense, it stems from behavior that is selfish; and that doesn't build a sense of togetherness and it doesn't build community.

The rugged individualist of nineteenth-century America, the gutsy soul who dared face the challenges of the dangerous West, had to have strength, courage, and determination. But it doesn't mean he faced the challenges of the West in isolation. Except for the few mountain men, the Western migration was a family migration; and it soon became a communal migration as towns and villages dotted the landscape. Hearty souls, yes. Souls in isolation, no. Only a fool or the wicked live with no thought to the greater good of the people around them. God made us to live in connection with himself and with others. In communal relationships we experience the best life can offer.

NEIGHBORS

Better a neighbor nearby than a brother far away.
—Proverbs 27:10c

My two brothers were my best friends growing up. We worked in Dad's construction business and farmed together. We hunted game and traipsed stream banks looking for antiques. We played baseball together. One year in Babe Ruth all three of us played on the same team; Bob at second base, Jim at shortstop, and me at third. Three of us, right in a row, with our sister Carol cheering from the stands. Our solidarity continued right into college when we all three of us attended Freed-Hardeman University for one year together.

But things changed. Graduation, jobs, marriage, and moving away placed us great distances from each other.

There is sadness in growing up and moving away, but that has always happened and always will. You miss the close camaraderie you once enjoyed together. I suppose it really can't be helped.

Fortunately God brings other people into our lives who function like family and who even become family. In the absence of Jim and Bob, I have enjoyed golf, hunting, fishing, baseball, and a host of other guy activities with Bennie, Taff, Dub, George, Marion, Elbert, Herb, Bob, Kirby, Kenny, Gary, Pete, Mike, Tracy, Jason, Rick, Lendy, Brian, Carl, John, David, and Keith, just to name a few. These neighbors nearby function in a way that a brother far away cannot. Better a neighbor nearby than a brother far away.

What is the function of a brother or a neighbor nearby? They give us a sense of camaraderie. Whether chasing a raccoon through the woods, hiking a mountain trail, cheering at a ball game, sitting in a hospital waiting room, or seeking advice on a family issue, we are sharing life with these brothers and neighbors. We are reminded and assured that we share both the joyous times and the painful ones with other people who care. We are not alone.

Secondly, they give us a sense of identity. I think I know who I am. I have identity. But that sense of identity is positively reinforced by those people who value me. These people spend time sharing in my moments of joy or pain. They remind me that I am valued either in the excitement of the sporting event or the sadness and fear of the waiting room.

Thirdly, they help us. No matter how strong we are, or think we are, none of us can stand totally alone in all the circumstances of life. It is hard to coach a team alone. It is hard to parent alone. It is hard to endure the struggles of life without a loving spouse by our side. On the other hand, it is a blessing to have people in our lives to encourage us when we feel like giving up and to hold up our hands when we are too weary to go on.

Finally, friends and neighbors give us a positive sense of eternity. Throughout the Bible, from Genesis to Revelation, friendship and fellowship are celebrated by God and his people. God even had a special sacrifice known as the "fellowship offering" where a man who felt blessed could sacrifice a bull, offer part of it to God, and offer the rest of it to his neighbors. They would gather around a table holding a feast and sharing in the joy of the blessed man. After his resurrection Jesus enjoyed a banquet with two of his followers (Luke 22:30). Jesus pictures the culmination of our human existence with a common meal shared by God with his people who heed his invitation (Luke 14). Cherished friendship today is a taste of the friendship, the banquet, and the celebration that we will share in eternity.

Sure, I still miss my brothers and sister and wish they were not so geographically distant. I would love to enjoy snowmobiling or hiking with them again. But I take to heart the counsel of Proverbs: Better a neighbor nearby than a brother far away. Good neighbors fill a gap in our lives when family is away.

AS IRON SHARPENS IRON

As iron sharpens iron, so one man sharpens another.
—Proverbs 27:17

Two boys differed profoundly. One was a shepherd boy; the other was royalty. One was the servant to the king; the other was son to the king. One was an invited guest in the royal palace; the other belonged there. But they also had some commonality between them which produced a close bond. They were both about the same age. They were both warriors. They both fought for Yahweh. They both, at times, trembled in the presence of the king. But most of all, they had a profound love and respect for the other. The first boy was named David; the other was named Jonathan.

1 Samuel 18:3 says that Jonathan made a covenant with David "because he loved him as himself." Jonathan, the son of the king, gave David, a servant of the king, his own robe, tunic, sword, bow, and belt. The servant would dress like a son. This covenant of friendship was reaffirmed and expanded upon with Jonathan declaring, "We have sworn friendship with each other in the name of the Lord" (1 Sam. 20:16, 42).

This reaffirmation of Jonathan's regard for David comes at a critical juncture in their story: Jonathan's father has already tried to kill David. Jonathan doesn't know at first that his father wants David dead. He hears what David has told him, but he has a hard time believing his father is conspiring to kill his best friend. So they set up a plan to draw Saul's intent out into the open. It works. Saul says, "David must die!" Jonathan, confused and hurt, bids his friend good-bye. He offers words of comfort: "The Lord is witness between you and me, and between your descendants and my descendants forever." The friends part.

This story has a sad ending. Jonathan fades from view now. Pretty much everything now is about David. Jonathan dies and David grieves (2 Sam. 1:25–27a), leaving David at center stage. David survives Saul's murderous attempts and goes on to become king. He conquers enemy nations and builds a kingdom that outlasts him by generations. He writes Psalms that memorialize him forever. But don't forget the contributions of the man who helped make David. Jonathan was a friend when David didn't have one. Jonathan risked his life to deliver his friend from danger. Jonathan bid farewell to his best friend in the world so his best friend could flee to safety.

Jonathan was struck down in the prime of his life. But his young life, well lived, made a lasting impression on David. His integrity, his character, and his truthfulness with his friend helped shape the life of the friend that eventually shaped the life of the entire nation. There might never have been a David if there hadn't been a Jonathan. David was the hero, but Jonathan was the tool that shaped him. "As iron sharpens iron, so one man sharpens another."

Who sharpened you in life? Who in your life has encouraged you, shaped you, and molded you in such a way that you are better because of them? Who has taken the time to love you and teach you? Who has loved you enough to risk losing you by giving you needed rebuke and scolding? Who has been the iron to shape you into the iron you have become?

Who are you sharpening? Who in your life are you encouraging, shaping, and molding in such a way that they are better because of you? Who are you taking the time to love and teach? Who do you love enough that you risk losing them by giving them needed rebuke and scolding? To who are you the iron that is shaping them into iron?

"As iron sharpens iron so one man sharpens another." Iron sharpens iron through friction. Friction existed between Jonathan and David. But it was because of the friction that this relationship became meaningful. If you sense friction in some of the relationships in your life, that might not be bad. That, in fact, might be very good. God may be working in that relationship to shape someone for good, either you or the other person.

As iron sharpens iron, so we are shaped by others, and others are shaped by us. Just be careful. Do you know who is shaping you and into what? Do you know who you are shaping and what they will become because of the experience? Let's make sure the influence we are under or the influence we are asserting is molding a life that will reflect the character of God.

FEAR OF MAN

Fear of man will prove to be a snare, but whoever trusts in the Lord is kept safe.

—Proverbs 29:25

The veins in his neck bulged. His face flushed. He breathed in short, violent gulps. He slammed his Bible on the desk shouting, "We have to get this right!"

The issue that inflamed this man was not central to faith or salvation. Although most would consider his concern a peripheral issue, this man was ready to fight with the preacher, sever relationships, possibly even split the church.

I wanted to deal with this man on the basis of his anger. But as I was to learn, just as the theological issue this man was ready to fight over was not a core issue, neither was anger his core issue. Underlying his external anger was deep internal fear. I don't know how the fear developed. It could have been a weak relationship with his father, early failures in his life, or family problems.

Fear hinders our relationships with others. Fear of other people often pushes us to automatically assume a defensive posture toward them. One such posture is avoidance. If we avoid other people, they can't hurt us. They can't belittle us, control us, or take advantage of us. If fear drives us to avoid others, we can't be hurt by a boyfriend or girlfriend and we can't be devastated by a divorce. Avoidance seems safe.

Another defensive posture is rudeness. A fearful person uses curt speech and unkind behavior to keep others at arm's length. A fearful person assumes, "If I hurt your feelings, you will not like me so you will stay away from me. Then, you can't hurt me." Rude and offensive people are usually very lonely. Really, rudeness is another form of avoidance, just more obnoxious.

One other defensive posture is control. The fearful person seeks to control the behavior of others so they can't hurt him. He wants others to talk and act in ways that he approves. Individuality is prohibited; not even personal thoughts or opinions are allowed because they threaten the self-image and equilibrium of the fearful controller. His inability to control his anxiety within drives him to control the anxiety external to him: other people. This is yet another form of avoidance. By controlling thoughts and behavior of others, he avoids genuine relationship with them.

Genuine relationship with other people means sharing ideas, acting together, even disagreeing on minor and major issues. Being in intimate connection with others runs the risk of hurting and being hurt by them, seeking and extending forgiveness. It means rearranging one's perceptions and plans to relate with others. In the most intimate form of relationship, marriage and connection mean surrendering one's will as an individual for the greater health of the relationship.

People fearful of other people struggle their whole lives with relationships. The thought of trusting another and surrendering their will strikes terror in their hearts. They can't think of sharing, giving, changing, and becoming one with another. They fear that they might lose who they are in a relationship with another. Therefore, they hide their insecurity from others and work hard to protect their image of being secure and strong. To do that, they practice avoidance, rudeness, and control.

Fear of man is a snare. It creates insecure feelings about ourselves and destabilizes our relationships with others. Only trust in the Lord empowers us to live to our full potential as human beings, secure in the knowledge that God creates us, loves us, and keeps us safe. A person with such inner confidence is not driven to avoid, be rude, or control others. Instead, he can interact with others through loving acceptance, even if they don't share total agreement.

SHE OPENS HER ARMS TO THE POOR

A wife of noble character who can find? She is worth far more than rubies . . . She opens her arms to the poor and extends her hands to the needy.

—Proverbs 31:10 and 20

One trait of a godly woman that makes her of such high character is that her heart can be stirred by the needs of people. It may be the needs of her husband, her children, or even other people that stir her; yet she is ready to lend a compassionate hand. If you've had such a noble woman as a mother or wife, you know the joy she brings to you and others.

When do such noble qualities as sharing and caring begin in life? When does the noble woman learn to open her arms to the poor and extend her hands to the needy? After she is married? As her children start coming into the world?

Healing Hands International (www.hhi-aid.org) is an organization that raises relief items for people all over the world. One time it sent nine forty-foot containers of relief items to the country of Ukraine to be distributed by churches. Included in this shipment were new baby incubators for the Gorlovka Children's Hospital.

Furthermore, Healing Hands helped the victims of the tsunami in Southeast Asia. In addition to sending food, Helping Hands assisted in repairing hundreds of damaged boats and purchased hundreds of new boats so that the fishermen could ply their trade and supply food to their people.

When one young lady from Jonesboro, Arkansas, Abbey, heard about the devastation to Southeast Asia, she was moved to donate money to help the victims. Although she had been saving money for a pair of Rollerblades, she decided that helping the victims was more important. So she planned to donate half of her saved money. In her own words, Abbey wrote to Healing Hands, "I heard what happened. I am send half my saving to you. From: Abbey."

If this seems like elementary writing, it is. Abbey was only seven years old when she wrote that letter. In a letter accompanying Abbey's donation, her mom wrote, "I am sending this check for my seven-year-old daughter, Abbey. One afternoon she was watching her TV and saw a report on the tsunami. She collected all of the money that she had been saving for a new pair of Rollerblades and brought it to her Dad. She said that she wanted to give it to the people who lost their home in the tsunami so they could build new homes. She wrote in her card that she was giving half of her savings: however, when she gave me the card that she made, she included all of her money. Needless to say, her father and I are extremely blessed to have her as a daughter" (Healing Hands International News, Volume 2005, Issue 1).

When does a godly woman learn to open her arms to the poor and extend her hands to the needy? After she is married? As her children are coming into the world? How about when she is seven years old? Actually, I'm sure the process began even years before, when young Abbey watched her mom and dad give generously to help people in need. It began when she heard their prayers for God to ease the hurt and suffering of others. It began when she saw her mom and other ladies from church take food to shut-ins.

"A wife of noble character who can find? She is worth far more than rubies . . . She opens her arms to the poor and extends her hands to the needy." The wife of noble character was first a little girl of noble character.

Someday when Abbey is an adult and she sees people who are suffering, it won't be any surprise to people who know her that she jumps in and helps. She will be a woman of noble character because she is a little girl of such character . . . character that is blessed with God's approval.

INDEX

Get Published, Inc!
Thorofare, NJ 08086
23 September 2009
BA2009266